BUSINESS
Missions
Accomplished

Silly Travel Tales on the Corporate Dime

Tim Jenkins

BUSINESS MISSIONS ACCOMPLISHED

Silly Travel Tales on the Corporate Dime

Copyright © 2020 Tim Jenkins

ISBN-13: 978-0-9998815-6-9

This book describes the author's experiences while traveling – on the road, in the air, at sea and through life events, mostly for business purposes – and reflects his opinions of those experiences. Some names and details have been changed to protect privacy, add cohesion, and to entertain.

If you enjoy <u>Business Missions Accomplished</u>, please leave a review on Amazon and consider reading its predecessors: <u>Missions Accomplished</u>, and <u>More Missions Accomplished</u>. Learn more about the author at: missionsaccomplishedpress.com

To road warriors and travelers everywhere – you are ambassadors to the world. Go everywhere you can, learn of other places, peoples, and cultures. Be nice. Eat a lot of really great food. Return home and tell of your adventures.

ACKNOWLEDGMENTS

This third book in the Missions Accomplished series was again boosted and bettered by the excellent work of others:

Carol Marks, Editing

Jefferson Adams, Narrative Coach

Heather Workman, Cover Art

Larry the bunny

And my cadre of story critics – you know who you are – many of whom have traveled with me, and some still willing to do so again in the future.

Where to next?

CONTENTS

Enjoy the journey!

Prelude: Business Unusual

"Travel is fatal to prejudice, bigotry, and narrow-mindedness."   – Mark Twain

A co-worker once framed it thus: "If I have to sling my ass on another plane this month, my wife will kill me. Better off dead, I suppose."

That's the mixed bag of the road warrior. It's all exertion, exhaustion and bleary-eyed jetlagged meetings. Except when it's glamorous passages to exotic cities and delectable cuisine at dinner.

There are – scientists have confirmed – four modes of voluntary travel: business, pleasure, business *and* pleasure, and expatriate life. Lucky me, to have experienced all these. *Involuntary* modes include – being trafficked, deported, refugee exodus, and boarding a vehicle headed the wrong way. Again, I'm lucky to have experienced only the latter two.

The tales herein document a few of my business adventures, most on the road, all a wild ride. Companies paid good money so I could live adventures on five continents. They let me keep the frequent flier miles. Being paid to travel is a great privilege. I'm grateful for the places I've seen, the quirky characters I've met, and the lessons learned. Being corporate ambassador is an honor, and a whole lot of fun.

Even when things don't go 100% as planned. They never do. Read on and see what I mean.

Bon voyage!

DEAD RECKONING

XIAN, CHINA

Terracotta Navigators

For the first and only time in all my travels, I found myself gripping the little white bag from the seat pocket in front of me, for its intended purpose. Stuck on the tarmac at Hongqiao airport, Shanghai, I willed the pilot into the air before things turned ugly.

Nausea was a black gully churning of toothed beasts in the pit of my stomach. It had been another night of excesses. When was I going to grow up and stop the madness? I'd still not learned my lesson when it came to business drink-a-thons with my Chinese business cohort. It was my own damn fault, as always. This was not my first or even thirty-first round of euphoric glass-held-high *gam bei* affairs that typically applied the exclamation mark to a successful week of sales in the People's Republic.

"Tim," Wa Ching had implored me last night, his face tomato red, tiny saké style cup nearly hidden in his beefy child-smooth hand. He raised it high above his head. He was built like a major household appliance, a rotund and jolly durable good, and given his surname of "Ma" – Wa Ching Ma -- we fell to calling him "Washing Machine."

"Tim. You…are…strong…drinker!"

Those would normally have been fighting words. I do my job, sure. Never let the customer drink alone. Yet I knew my limit was somewhere close at hand. Converting that knowledge into common sense was not my forte'.

The reptilian portion of my brain commandeered my hand, boosted the cup high overhead, and met Wa Ching's with a loud "thunk." We both broke into chortles as the expensive Mou Tai splashed onto our fingers. The aroma as we went "bottoms-up" was akin to turpentine. The taste, though, was saucy-sweet and beguiling. It re-burnt a well-worn trail down my esophagus with soothing heat and invigorating spice. It truly warmed the heart, and therein lay the danger.

The alarm had blasted me out of bed pre-dawn, and the scramble for the airport had masked the sorry state of my system. An injury of my own making, my philosophy is to maximize the value of each trans-oceanic crossing. Having flown "the pond" my goal was to see every customer possible, and pack the schedule to overflowing, in alignment with the Road Warrior's creed: meet customers in their lair, make it easy for them, take them to lunch, dinner, breakfast, drinks at the pub. Provide an indispensable service, a sound – if over-hyped – product, candid communications, and a warm bond, the latter being the most formidable competitive moat ever deployed on the business battlefield.

The plane to Xian was scheduled before sun-up. I left the hotel in darkness and had only a dim memory of doing my usual lightning check after zipping my backpack closed. The challenge is to ensure nothing is left behind in the room but a few well-earned *kuai* for the maid. Two items scare me most when changing cities: my passport and laptop charger. The rest is readily replaceable or foregone. The certainty of a new toothbrush in every hotel room in Asia made me lazy in regard to toiletries.

The taxi ride to the airport, the passage through security and the wait at the gate were a blur. It was when the plane slowly taxied that I noticed my discomfort had evolved into queasiness and then erupted into full-fledged resistance of the urge.

Sunlight barely infused the clouds as the plane sped down the runway, rotated, and leapt into the sky. The pilot applied maximum thrust and lift, and the acceleration acted as a momentary salve. The quicker at altitude, the sooner the seat belt light would be extinguished. Even though passenger conduct in China was anything but FAA conforming in those days, I didn't want to jump out of my seat at an inopportune moment.

Gingerly, I pulled the air sickness bag from the pocket and experimented with the white tab that facilitated its opening and its crude sealing after the deed. The pre-projectile vomit warnings were peaking again as the plane started to level off well after the 10,000 foot chime had sounded. "Never again," echoed in my skull. This time, no question, I meant it.

The pit of void monsters in my gut were apparently emboldened by my predicament. Next to me was a prepossessing young woman reading the in-flight magazine, and across the aisle was an observant Ah Ma who eyed me and my little white bag with great curiosity. I really did not want to use the blasted thing, but the monsters raced, faster, faster, and now they meant to surface.

DING.

I broke the latch of my lap belt and exploded out of the seat. The lavatory was just paces behind. I gargled back the acidic stew of last night's feast, bolted the door and flung open the lid. I had mere seconds to spare as I aimed and let her rip.

Despite the rattling of the lavatory door as we hit an air pocket, my aim was true. A direct hit. Then another, then a third. Oh, what a feeling! It was like being reborn. I washed, wiped, scrubbed, flushed, primmed, finger-combed, gargled with airline faucet water. I breathed in. I exhaled. Survival presented itself as a distinct possibility. More good news, I had avoided making a mess as I had done at my bachelor's party, an act my best man's wife had never forgiven, nor should she.

As I settled back into my airline seat, giving my seatmates a polite and calming nod, I realized the monsters were not done with me. A few continued to skulk down below, and the grunge grew. I had cast their brethren out and they seemed intent on settling the score at a time of their choosing.

Long after our plane landed in Xian and I'd reached my hotel, they persisted. Washing Machine had wisely taken a later flight, allowing him to sleep-in to a more civilized hour, yet now he was suddenly downstairs, calling me on the house phone. "We meet in lobby now," he said.

I'd collapsed onto the hotel bed and drifted into post-vomit purgative sleep. Now, still shaky, I was also late. I scrambled to pull it together.

Wa Ching reclined in the shotgun position as our driver sped from the hotel. I sprawled in the backseat. Soon our car was whipping along a lonely multi-lane highway, dry yellow sands receding in all directions. Wa Ching's snores were lulling, and after ensuring I'd applied the seat belt correctly, I too drifted, my eyes flickering open, not wanting to miss the grandeur of the desert.

Not far away, Xian's famous terracotta warrior statues beckoned, and I had hopes that my stomach gremlins and the customer's brevity might open the window for Wa Ching and I to see them before that bucket-list exhibition closed for the evening. My flight to Shenzhen was 6:15am tomorrow, so now or never. I drifted into sleep.

It's a cardinal rule of sales in China that foreigners not reveal their schedule when meeting a customer for the first time. Doing so undermines one's negotiation position, and I aspire to respond to these inquiries with ambiguity.

Doubly key in this instance, as I'd be meeting my Xian sales counterpart – James – for the first time, as well as his most cherished customer, a high-ranking procurement officer of the People's Liberation Army (PLA). It's widely understood that the PLA is the second branch of Chinese government. Their procurement power overshadows the likes of Huawei and SinoChem, with clout sufficient to make or break vendors with their purchasing whims. My tiny company had many customers across the globe. While losing a PLA contract wouldn't break us, winning would be a game changer. James was the face of that customer, and what a face.

Still groggy from my nap, I let James hug me as

we entered the customer's lobby. My height, he was atypically wide. True, I was diminished by last night's excesses, yet his squeeze felt like the death-grip of an Anaconda. Behind his coke-bottle dark-rimmed glasses, his eyes sparkled.

"You are a beast!" he said. "So strong!" Why he said this, I don't know, since I could hardly draw breath under his constrictor squeeze.

"It's a pleasure," I told him, putting our relationship on a higher plane than my roiling gut and acute muscular pain.

James's smile was priceless. Once he finally ended the agony by releasing me, I was able to return the smile. Then he spun me sideways, and pulled my ear close to his mouth. I only hoped my breath was not as foul as the tobacco and alcohol aroma that accompanied his whisper. I felt my digestive demons roil.

"Tim," he said breathily. "We can *win* this one. Do you know how many soldiers in the PLA?"

Of course I did. I mean, I love Trivial Pursuit, and had never forgotten the night that my friend Jake had made us all wait for twelve minutes while he had counted up all the soldiers in all the standing armies in the world, which was what the game card had asked of him. It annoyed the hell out of me and our friends as he dithered, calculated, and ascribed fractional multiples to the global population, and then methodically focused in on the most militaristic nations on the planet at the time – the USSR, USA, Iraq and Iran, Vietnam, North Korea, and finally China.

Jake had then stated with confidence "Twenty-five million," and earned our unending annoyance by getting it exactly right, which sparked an argument about whether he had read all 5,000 questions and answers before we'd sat down to play.

"Two million," I informed James.

His smile vanished, replaced with a grimace of disdain. "Yes. That's close." The smile returned, and he slapped my shoulder. "Think about it! Every soldier in the PLA wearing a watch with our sensor cluster. We'll be rich!" His eyes lit up. "I'll be rich!" he corrected. He was a reseller, after all, with open-ended mark-up front and center in his contract.

An entourage of young, uniformed soldier procurement agents ushered us into a large conference room. The colonel entered the room. He was smiling, gracious, polite and under-stated. He listened to James pontificate about our sensor cluster, proprietary ASIC, and patented inertial measurement algorithms, which he assured the colonel would put every combatant soldier in the right place at the right time, a war-winning combo.

"Our technology," said James, "will position each soldier facing in the correct direction, accurate to one degree, give or take a few arc minutes based on the presence of soft-iron interference, a common result of proximity to armored vehicles, like our nation's finest tanks." Jesse had parroted the caveat on our company's datasheet.

The colonel sat gently smiling while I walked him through our company overview slides and technology roadmap. He asked only one question.

"Do you like Chinese food?"

I ignored the uplift of gut monsters at this mention of gastronomy and answered with an enthusiastic affirmation. The colonel clapped his hands jauntily and made it clear that there would be a banquet for dinner, featuring the finest Mou Tai turpentine liquor, and charming young ladies to dance with, immediately following the meeting. It was nearly 5:00pm, and the terracotta soldiers were fading along with my stamina.

"*Hǎo*," I told him. "Great." I then tried to back-pedal with courteous yet spirited humility that this was too much, so inconvenient for him, and I didn't want to keep him from his family.

James leapt from his chair, pinched my bicep, and informed me: "No problem, the colonel's family lives in Beijing. He is free tonight! So are we! I want nothing more than to ***drink hard*** with you, with you and the colonel!"

Washing Machine suddenly seemed to awaken from his slump. "Tim…is…strong…drinker!"

I bid good-bye to the dream of ever seeing the terracotta warriors, and I hoped they shed a tear for me as I was swooped away with James on my left – occasionally torturing my bicep with an affectionate pinch – and the colonel on my right, in the backseat of the colonel's limo. At first, I feared the rise of my gastric sea-devils. Soon, I slowly came to realize that they, too, were tired. I began to suspect they were even a little scared. They left me alone as we dined on turtle, scorpion, duck and bullfrog, all very nicely seasoned, and drowned in the most delusive Mou Tai.

After settling into the nightclub, the colonel asked, "Tim, what time is your flight tomorrow?"

"Flight?" I asked, as always striving for ambiguity on this key point of short schedule. "But colonel, why would I ever want to leave Xian?"

The colonel grinned broadly. "Wa Ching says

you are a strong drinker." Wa Ching was not there at the moment as, battling his own demons, he had nearly upchucked onto one of the fetching entertainers, much to the colonel's delight, and was now passed out on an immense lounge sofa.

"Not at all, colonel," I said. "He's much stronger." The colonel belted out a laugh, pointing to where Wa Ching was lying on his back, hands draped over his generous belly.

"Let's now see," said the colonel, "who is strongest of all." He gave me a playful wink. I decided it would be good for business to let him win. He had a great time, and after I surrendered, he, too, passed out cold. Maybe Washing Machine was right. Maybe I *am* a strong drinker. I should probably add that to my LinkedIn profile.

We didn't get the big deal. As I flew out of Xian, a few beaten down hydrochloric dragons still circling in my gut, I sensed the mocking laughter of 5,000 Neolithic terracotta warriors enjoying a good gut-bust at my expense in their cool caves below that vast sea of inner Mongolian dust.

SHUTTERSTOCK

TAIPEI, TAIWAN

Halcyon Daze

"Wake up, sir," said a voice. "*Please*. We don't need another DOA coming off this flight."

Who was talking? Were they talking to *me*? There were bright lights and a powerful squeeze on my shoulder. Ouch! Against my better instinct, I battled open first my right eye-lid, then my left. I was on the plane. Which plane?

I looked toward the aisle. A very charming smile greeted my gaze. She had sparkling eyes and long black hair in cornrows.

"You're ok, honey," she said. "We landed. Take your time. I just wanted to make sure you were ok. *Are* you ok?"

With no clue why she was asking, or even the honest response to her question, I forced my mouth open. An opposing force, exerted by the cement that had formed from my dried spittle, battled my jaw muscles. I managed to croak out. "Good."

"That's good," she said with enthusiasm. Then she turned to look behind me, down the aisle of the aircraft in which I'd awoken, and which I realized must have landed at least ten minutes ago, since I couldn't see anybody seated, nor standing, in the many rows of the aircraft ahead of me.

"This one's fine," she shouted over my shoulder.

It was good to know I was fine and I'd arrived. Where, exactly, didn't feel too important. I sensed I'd remember any moment now. I could take my time. Well, no, I needed to get off this plane, because I was the last passenger. And I needed to complete a slide deck before morning.

With gathering strength, I found the buckle of my seat belt, felt a sense of pride once it finally clicked open, and began to stand up. Ouch again. Using both arms to steady myself, I slowly came to stand almost erect. I took a deep breath. What's next?

I swiveled to look toward the back of the aircraft. I wanted to catch another glimpse of the damsel who'd (in my imagination) kissed me back to life. I meant to thank her, but she and a colleague were very busy right now leaning over the only other passenger on the aircraft. Chad.

Chad? How did I know his name? He sat, aisle seat, ten rows back, mouth wide open, eyes shut, as if he were trying to capture snowflakes streaming down from a winter sky. My savior reached him and his mop of thick blond hair was vibrating as she gave him the same jolting squeeze action back-and-forth that I'd just received.

Then it hit me. Chad was dead. She'd said DOA. Dead On Arrival! Dear god! Was it my fault? Holy crap. Think, brain! What had happened?

******

"Hey, man, can you snag me one of those?" said a twenty-something gentleman who chatted me up in the terminal bookstore at LAX. I was grabbing the Wall Street Journal. He'd held a Tom Clancy paperback and had asked me to reach a Sports Illustrated magazine for him.

"Dude," he said, "you should get one, too. Swimsuit edition!" His blond hair, tanned face, and Valley Guy inflection indicated he likely spent time catching waves at Zuma, Malibu, and Redondo.

I laughed. "Have you read any other Clancy books?" I asked.

"No, dude, I heard he's good. Lots of spy shit, right?"

I nodded. "That too. Tense diplomacy, secret government plots, real-world CIA kinds of adventures."

"Awesome. I dig that 007 shit." There was a line to check out. He stood behind me in the queue. "Dude, I'm Chad." I turned and returned the courtesy. "So, hey," he asked, "where you flyin' today?"

"Taiwan," I informed him. "You?"

"Same flight, man! Cool, hey we got time to burn. Let's say we get a few beers over there." He pointed across the terminal walkway to a pre-flight burrito shop with bar. The gate was close by, and we had 30 minutes. I saw no harm.

We bellied up to the bar. "Foster's on draft, dude!" said Chad. "Far out!"

"That sounds good." I ordered a pint. "And whatever this gentleman is having."

"Hey, thanks, bud, you havin' just one? I go double whammy before a flight. That's not even a super-sizer!"

A 15 hour non-stop flight to Taipei. In economy class. I found it difficult to brush Chad's logic aside. "Supersize me," I said. The barkeep laughed.

"Yeah," said Chad. "And I'll have *two* of what he's having."

It wasn't cheap. Still, it was a good idea to hydrate and relax. Yes, yes, beer is a diuretic in sheep's clothing, but the logic of its cold bubbly amber is unstoppable. I planned to sleep as much as possible on the flight, sticking to my eat, work, sleep, eat, work, arrive progression that is my standard for trans-Pacific hauls.

Beers in hand, we made our way to a table. "Cheers!"

We enjoyed the first quaff, of which mine was finished while Chad's was still picking up steam. "So, what takes you to Tai—"

Chad's mug hit the table so hard, I thought something was wrong. His blue eyes were wide, he wiped his arm across his mouth. "Shit, man, that tastes good! Whewweee!"

It was good beer. I couldn't help but be impressed that his supersized mug was now nearly half empty. "So, what's your—"

"No way, man," he said. "I want to know your story first. You going for fun and sun like me?"

"Not quite," I admitted. "Work. Plus, I'm visiting my wife."

His grin seriously widened. He looked like a happy shark about to swallow a seal whole. "Whoa, dude, you got a babe there?"

"OK," I laughed. "Sure, you can say that. She's from Taoyuan City. We got married last year, and her family is there. So she's spending a couple months visiting. And I'm visiting her – and them – for a week, plus calling on customers for my company."

Chad nodded his head enthusiastically while taking another slug of beer. The mug came down just as loudly. "Dude, Taoyuan City? Like, is that close to Bangkok?"

I had to think about that. The two cities are probably 1200 kilometers (750 miles) or more apart and in different countries. Uh, oh, I thought.

"No, no," I said. "Taoyuan City is where we're going to land. It's where the Taipei International airport is. You did say you're going to Taiwan, right?"

"Totally, man. I can't wait. Tell me how you found your wife. Did you just hit the beach at Pattaya and they swarmed on you? That's what happened to my buddy."

This was downright awkward. Pattaya was a famous party beach south of Bangkok. In Thailand. Not Taiwan.

"Nothing like that," I said. "I was teaching English and I met her at a party. She wanted English lessons but, well you know, when she turned me down due to cost, I had to turn to Plan B. I asked if she'd consider teaching me Chinese instead of paying me. A mutual language lesson exchange."

Chad was giggling. "Oh, man, you snared her! Great job, buddy."

Come to think of it, I guess I had. "I got lucky, for sure. The Taiwanese really want to learn English. The Chinese are very business focused, and you and I are lucky enough to speak the most important business language as natives." I studied his face closely, hoping for signs of recognition that he was about to fly to Taiwan. Not Thailand.

"Man, that's so cool," he said, then took the first swig from his second supersized Fosters. "I can't wait to hang at the beach bars at Pattaya and connect with the babes."

I drew a deep breath. Lots of Americans are weak in geography, as if they'd never been exposed to a world map or globe in their lives. It often went beyond simple ignorance to the utterly absurd. I thought I'd heard and seen it all. There are Americans who talk about Africa as a single country, almost as big as Texas (not the continent that is three times bigger than the entire continental United States and home to more than 100 nations) and others who 'know' for a fact that Taiwan is the largest city in Japan. Many think Puerto Rico is a foreign country.

I'd read a news story as a teenager about a man who boarded an airplane in Los Angeles. The flight was bound for Auckland, New Zealand. On landing the man had been very confused and complained to the airline: "You put me on the wrong plane! I bought a ticket for Oakland!" He hadn't. He'd paid way too much for a ticket to Oakland, California. He just wasn't paying attention and had no idea there might be a city somewhere else in the world with a name that sounded a bit like Oakland -- Auckland. The airline performed good customer service by feigning embarrassment, refunding him the ticket price, and sending him back to California first-class on the next flight.

I'd had plenty of folks ask me to clarify: was my new wife from Thailand? No, I had to explain. She's Chinese and from Taiwan, the Republic of China.

Some were good with that and knew that Taiwan was an island nation independent (more or less, depending on who you were arguing with) and off the south coast of China. Some required more information.

I hated to be the one to burst his bubble, but it was clear to me that Chad had no idea that he was flying to the wrong country. Still, I might be misinterpreting him. "So, are you planning a trip to Thailand soon?"

"Sure," he said, "if I have a blast this time, I'll probably head back in a month or two. I've got lots of vacation time."

I dreaded what I must do next. It seemed my duty to inform Chad that he was boarding a plane to Taiwan. Not Thailand. This would not be easy. Don't ask me why, but my mind flashed back to the pivotal climactic scene of the movie, *Old Yeller*, when the young boy must put down his one and only dearest friend, his dog. My throat parched a little, so I took a quick swig to moisten the pipes, and cleared my throat.

"So, Chad, you know—"

His ears perked-up. "Dude," he said, "that's us. They're starting to board. Hey, really appreciate the beers, man. Here, let me give you this." He took out a small white plastic container from the rear pocket of his backpack. "Got to get these out, anyway. I'm going to sleep like a baby on this flight." He handed me two bluish colored pills.

"What are these?"

He flashed the bottle's label so I could see. "Halseeon, dude. They will tranquilize your ass. You won't even know you were flying. Just take these after dinner and…poof! You'll wake up in old Siam."

"Oh, thanks." I said, thinking, ok, no connecting flight. He did not have a clue. "Really, I'm ok, thanks. You know—"

"Come on, man," he said. "At least take one. Keep it! I'll take this one back, never know, I might need three to get max rested and ready for those Pattaya babes!"

I relented, since he was already packing up. I dropped the pill into my shirt pocket. I still intended to let Chad know that his destination was the Republic of China, and not Thailand, but he suddenly bolted and shouted over his shoulder. "Dude, see you onboard. Maybe see you there, too. Bangkok, baby! The most appropriately named city in the world! Wooooeeee!"

Well, that was a perspective, and not one unhitched from reality. But he wasn't *going* to Bangkok. Was he? I should have tried to see his ticket.

Sure enough, onboard, I saw Chad seated ten or more rows behind me. Before dinner I passed him on the way to the lav, but he was deep in conversation with a seatmate – a young woman whose flowing black hair and almond eyes led me to assume that she was visiting friends or family back in Taiwan. I figured by now he must know where he was really going.

Dinner was served. I worked an hour on my laptop, then tried to nap, but mostly fidgeted. There were eleven hours to go and I needed to sleep. The seat I'd been assigned was particularly uncomfortable, with a support blocking half of what should have been my ration of leg room. There was a movie rolling on the entertainment system, but it was a romantic comedy – I struggle with the genre.

What the heck. I took the little bluish pill from my shirt pocket and studied it closely. Halseeon. Chad had recommended two or maybe three. Still, I knew better than to take a strange pharmaceutical given by a stranger. I watched the movie, and built out some of the slides needed for tomorrow on my laptop. I endured the annoyance of discomfort, and waited for sleep.

In the meantime, my seatmate – a huge guy, who pound-for-pound was getting double the value out of his economy class ticket that I was – began to snore loudly. His head had bent onto his left shoulder, and thus pointed at close range directly into my right ear. Oh, crap. My resolve softened. A bit. I took one more hard look at the gift Chad had given me.

Screw it. I bit off half the pill and chased it with water. Half a pill – 25% the recommended dose. Then I got up to use the restroom and stretch, hoping to catch Chad. He was fast asleep, mouth open, two empty plastic cups on his tray, each adorned with an olive skewered by a decorative toothpick. His head was drooped rightward, pointed at the young woman whose eyes were staring aimlessly out the window.

******

That's the last I remembered. I must have made it back to my seat, gotten comfy, and plummeted into dreamland. It was coming back to me now as I walked down the empty cabin to more closely inspect my new friend, the last passenger still seated on this flight.

The attendant, my savior, had taken a break from shaking him awake. "He's ok," she said. "Breathing anyway. Your friend?"

"Just met him during pre-boarding. He gave me a pill."

"Halseeon, right?" she asked.

"Yes! I took half." I fished into my shirt pocket past my passport and presented the other half.

"Smart of you," she said, "not to do what he did. Your buddy took a lot more than that. We see this all the time. The manufacturer is cutting the dosage way back because of things like this. He's survived this far, so he'll be fine. He may not remember much, though."

She glanced over my shoulder. "Here they come. The calvary have arrived."

We stepped out of the aisle as two Taiwanese paramedics rolled a thin gurney down it. They loaded Chad's limp form up and wheeled him away. One was efficiently taking his blood pressure while they were in motion.

"Thanks for saving my life," I told her.

"That's nothing, honey," she said. "All in a day's work." Then she busied herself gathering up Chad's bags.

I found my own backpack and roller, and got off that plane. Good news about Chad, I thought. Not going DOA, that is. The flight attendant had mentioned memory loss. Maybe Chad would forget all about Bangkok and learn to love Taipei. It isn't 'the most appropriately named city in the world,' perhaps, but I knew from personal experience he would have no trouble finding "the babes" here.

When I threw open my laptop late that night, I looked up Halseeon. The manufacturer laid on lots of warnings regarding what one should and should

not do when taking it. It also advised "temporary amnesia is a common side-effect." Then I set about finishing my presentation slides, and immediately got yet another surprise.

They were already done. Somewhere between taking half a Halseeon and passing out, I'd finished my homework. The slides weren't bad, either. I guess preparing a sales pitch doesn't weigh-in the same as "operating a moving vehicle or heavy machinery."

NORTHERN CALIFORNIA

Blazing Passports

It was already 9:07am, and there was an elephant in the conference room. Worse, neither Blaze nor I was talking about the elephant. We were ignoring it, as humans tend to do.

Mike burst into the conference room, waving a blue booklet. "I wonder what dipshit left this in the break room," said Mike.

Blaze and I had half-heartedly been reviewing our pitch for the China seminar, which Blaze would deliver on Monday to a crowd of interested customers in Shanghai. Today was Friday. Our flight left from San Francisco tomorrow morning, and due to loss of 16 hours in time zones, arrived in Shanghai Sunday night. Monday 8:00am was game-on. We were almost out of time.

Our review of the material had been shallow at best, entirely due to our mutual distraction. My distraction was well-founded. On fear. Fear and foreboding. Fear and foreboding founded on the fact that Blaze could not seem to find his passport, and our flight would be "wheels-up" in 26 hours. Blaze's distraction was that he was busy trying to remember exactly where he'd last seen the dang thing.

Now Mike, like the *deus ex machina*, had strutted in waving what to all appearances was a well-worn United States Passport. "Mike," I said, "please don't tell us this is some kind of joke. Please tell us that's Blaze's passport."

"Well, now," said Mike. "How the fuck would I know? Oh, I see your point. Let me just open it and take a look." His sense of humor ran a close second to his sense of outrage. Both were now triggered and in gear. Blaze and I watched him dramatically lick his index finger and use it to flick open the thick, well-traveled booklet. "Hmm, what have we here? It's a photo of a guy who looks a lot like Blaze, back when he wasn't butt ugly, at least."

Blaze perked up like a penguin on parade, blazing his Blaze grin. "You're my personal hero! How did you find it?"

"In god's name," said Mike, "how do you *think* I found it? Your sidekick here," he gestured to me, "put out an 'all-points bulletin' to every employee that finding your passport was our top priority. So I found it. Sheesh."

"Mike," I said, "you're a hero indeed. Where was the blasted thing? We searched the whole freaking office last night and again this morning."

"Well," he said, "clearly you weren't looking very hard, now were you?"

"Can't argue with that," said Blaze, standing to receive his travel document, which Mike graciously surrendered to him. "Really, though, where?"

"Almost right where you left it," said Mike. "In the break room."

"No freaking way," I said. "We searched every

inch of that place."

"Really?" asked Mike, who now actually cracked a smile. "Really? Thorough search, eh? Checked all the nooks and crannies, did you?"

"I do kind of remember," said Blaze, "glancing at my passport in the break room on Tuesday while grabbing some tea. Now it's all coming back."

"Was it in the refrigerator?" I asked Mike.

"Getting warm!" he said. "But...no, too cold. It was *under* the refrigerator."

I slapped my forehead. "Of course. Blaze must have dropped it and then he or somebody kicked it underneath."

"You know," said Mike, "You're no Einstein, but that's a pretty fair hypothesis. I'll give you a point for that one."

"Thanks. But it completely begs the question," I pointed out. "How did you even think to look *under* the refrigerator?" I was braced and ready to be excoriated for asking such a dumb question, but my curiosity had the better of me at this point.

"Well," said Mike, "I could harp on my prior statement about being ordered to drop everything of importance and halt the entire company's productive work to go mindlessly searching for this fool's passport. Yet there's a little more to it than just that."

"Do tell!" encouraged Blaze.

"Well," said Mike, "you guys know I've got a very tight sphincter. Don't give me those scandalous looks! It's well established that I'm anal retentive."

"No argument there," I said.

"And you know where I get that?"

"I don't know," I said, "but could you rub some of that off on *him*?" and pointed to Blaze.

"Yeah, I'll take some of that," said Blaze. "I mean, I'll skip anything *directly* anal, but—"

"I got it from my father," said Mike. "Dad was a first-class wackadoodle, completely over the top. Kept the cleanest house anyone's ever seen. Drove my mother crazy. Did *this* to me," and Mike waved the fingers of both hands at himself from the shaggy mop of brown hair down past his sweatshirt to his ill-fitting blue jeans. "He meant well. He kept it clean. I'm talking like 'let's clean the garage again' every weekend clean. And you know what he did every morning when got up?"

"Brewed coffee?" I suggested.

"No, he was a tea drinker. He staggered into the kitchen at 5:45am every day, weekends and holidays included. And the first thing he did was to reach into the broom closet and grab his wooden meter stick. Then he ripped not one but two paper towels off the roll, wetted them, wrapped them around the stick. Then he crouched down next to the refrigerator and reached under it and used that stick to mop up every speck of dust that might have somehow snuck down there in the prior 24 hours. Sometimes he got a marble or a dead fly. He never did get a passport."

"Incredible," I said. "Thanks to your dad, Blaze is going to China."

"Well," said Blaze, "I *might* be going."

"What?" said Mike. "You'll damn well get on that plane. I didn't do all that scrounging for nothing."

"Well, sure, I will if I can."

"What now, Blaze?" I asked.

"Well, it's just that, I remember now that Mike has located my passport – and thank you very much!

– that I'd brought it to the break room. I was on a call, and needed tea, and while I was talking I was thinking that I should make sure I had a visa for China."

"Did you?" I asked. "Do you?"

"I do!"

"Ok, then."

"But, I think it might have expired." There was a loud exhalation sound. A sigh of disbelief. I think it came from yours truly. Mike and I watched in suspense as Blaze flipped through his worn passport.

"Oh, yep," said Blaze. "Expired last week. Well, no problem, I'll renew on arrival in Shanghai."

"Oh no," I said. "I don't think so. Mike, great job, I'll take it from here."

"And best of luck to you, Einstein." Mike gave a little bow and exited the conference room.

"Won't be a problem," said Blaze. "I've done it before."

"Yeah, yeah, sure," I said. "Tell me again how you did it before, and how you were detained for most of a day by Chinese Immigration, and were lucky to get into the country."

"Hey! You remember that story."

"I may be no Einstein, but I don't forget good travel disaster tales. Let's not create a new one. Let's call Skip." I looked at my watch. "Pre-10:00am, there's a shred of hope here."

Skip was the magician retained by my previous employer. He ran a travel agency that specialized in visas and travel documents on an urgent basis. Given that it was the start of travel season, I knew he'd be busy, but therefore in full fighting trim.

"Skip it is!" said Blaze as I rung him up on the

Polycom.

"Futuretravel," he answered on the first ring.

"Hi Skip, Tim here. Sounds like you're driving."

"No problem, hands free. How can I help?"

"My counterpart, technically my boss, Blaze, who's here with me now—"

"Hey, Skip!"

"…hi Blaze…"

"…has an expired China visa, which is the darndest thing, as we're off to Shanghai tomorrow."

"What day? Tomorrow? Oh, oh, I see. Oh. Oh OK." Skip was Chinese American. He spoke excellent Cantonese. I could hear him speaking it now, very loudly and quite quickly to someone who apparently was in the car with him. "OK, ok. No problem. We can do this. Blaze, how quickly can you meet us in San Francisco?"

"I'm just 70 minutes away," said Blaze. "Even less if you say so."

"No, no need for law-breaking," said Skip. "But we'll need you here by 11:45, before the consulate closes for lunch."

"I'm halfway there now!" said Blaze.

"Great," said Skip. "Do you have a current passport and two passport photos?"

"Well," said Blaze, "I can get the photos on my way there. And now, I've actually got a passport!"

He began flipping through it again, no doubt to ensure it was his actual passport, and not the fake "Elvis" passport he enjoyed carrying for purposes of humor, and which had played prominently in his near incarceration at the hands of Chinese Immigration the last time he'd used it in that country. It was, in a nutshell, the disaster tale in question, and manifested when Blaze had somehow accidentally gotten a new China visa in his Elvis passport and not in his actual passport. A mistake anyone could make; anyone who carries fake passports as a joke, that is.

"That's outstanding," said Skip. "Please write this address down." I scribbled it as he spoke, and began mapping it. "Start of summer, peak travel doc season, so please be on-time."

"Sixty-three minutes," I said. "Blaze is mounting up as we speak."

"Great," said Skip.

Blaze was still smiling as he lingered over his passport. "Oh, I'll beat that time handily. There is one more thing, though."

"One more?" said Skip. "Oh, yes, sorry, there will be an expedite fee on this."

"Oh, no problem there," I assured him.

"Yes," said Blaze, "no worries at all. Only one more thing I just noticed."

"Another thing?" asked Skip. "How I can help? Though, it might be best if you tell me while driving. We're really in a crunch here."

Oh, no, I thought. Please don't tell us--

"Looks like my passport is also expired," said Blaze. "Think you can help us with that?"

That elephant in the room? It was now rampaging. It had our full attention.

There was a sudden shout on the Polycom in Cantonese, a female voice, from Skip's car. I don't speak the language, but I thought this was not a joyful sound. I wasn't feeling joyful myself. If Blaze wasn't on the plane to Shanghai tomorrow, I'd be stuck holding the bag, a total novice trying to fake my way through a presentation before hundreds of customers who expected a rock-star, Blaze, with his 25 years industry experience.

"Skip," I said. "Come in, Skip. Are you reading us? Over!"

"Oh. Yes, one moment please." He shouted something in Cantonese. "I'm here. OK. I understand. When did your passport expire?"

"Three weeks ago," said Blaze. "Oh, that's weird. Now I'm wondering how I managed to fly out of Israel on an expired passport."

A loud thud assaulted my ears. I realized it was the sound of my face as it planted itself in my palm.

"Blaze," said Skip's voice over the Polycom. "You can be in San Francisco very quickly?"

"Super fast!"

"Are you a U.S. Citizen, Blaze?"

"All my life."

There was a whole lot more Cantonese. It sounded to me like Skip and his co-worker were thrashing about what to do with all this rapidly developing information. "Um, guys," said Skip. "You know passport renewals are backed-up this time of year. Give us just one moment."

"Take your time," said Blaze. "Not too long, though," as he glanced at his watch. I started slapping my face, none too gently, right hand right cheek, left hand left cheek. It didn't help, but Blaze laughed at the gesture. "Don't worry. Everything's working out fine!"

The voices from the Polycom grew more guttural, more distressed. Finally, Skip said: "Look, guys. My folks are holding a wad of 70, maybe 80 passports. We're racing to the consulate to get these folks China visas, too. Most of them are traveling

Monday but maybe a third are outbound Tuesday or later in the week. So, we're talking here about maybe we sit on those until Monday so we can double-team this situation."

"Great thinking," said Blaze.

I hit the mute button. "Dude this is going to cost." Unmute. "Skip, can you really do it?"

"Well, technically, it's not a physical impossibility. It's a bit of a ... what's that American football term, it's a bit of a Mary Hail."

"Hail Mary, full of grace!" said Blaze, who, like me, was a failed Catholic.

"We'll need to call in some favors at the U.S. desk," said Skip. "They really hate it when we do that. We've got an insider who might work through lunch to generate a new passport, strictly against the rules, so it's ...um...it's not easy. But, uh, maybe we can make this work. Fees will be, well, sorry. I can't generate a quote right now. They will be exceptional. Is that ok?"

"Oh, that's perfectly fine!" said Blaze.

"OK," said Skip. "And forget what I said about not breaking the law. We need to be very, very quick, meet me at the U.S. consulate pronto. Four photos, now, not just two. Blaze, are you driving yet?"

And with that, Blaze ejected out of his chair, grin wide as a mile. "I'm starting the engine now!" and he was gone. I looked to make sure the expired passport had gone out the door with him.

Then, I exhaled. "Skip, he's on his way. And if you guys can pull this off, I will personally hum the Notre Dame fight song in your honor."

"No need," said Skip. "Just forgive the size of invoice. It will exceed all expectations. Even mine."

Hail Mary, full of grace....

The next morning our flight to Shanghai left on time, with both Blaze and I onboard. Blaze had a shiny new passport with a spanking new China visa stamp, and a wholly unchanged rosy outlook on life. I'll always envy him for that.

"Skip is great," he said, as the plane rotated and lifted off the runway. "We got my new passport by 2:15, raced to the China Consulate, then I bought everyone hot dogs for lunch."

"You cheaped-out with hotdogs?" I asked.

"Mexican street dogs," Blaze clarified. "The best. Then, I completely made up for the fast-food lunch after the visa came through at 8:30pm. I took Skip and lots of people I didn't know to a fancy dinner in Chinatown."

"Awesome," I told Blaze. "The least you could do. Glad you're *my* boss and not the other way around. I'd hate to sign off on that expense report."

"Me, too!" he said. "Definitely a new record."

"Worse than your $1500 mobile phone bill last month?" The CEO had actually phoned Blaze on that one and asked him to reign it in a bit.

"Not much worse. What's $2490 in the big scheme? The good news is, we'll both be on another continent when Dutch finds my expense report on his desk Monday morning."

Our aircraft accelerated up and away from our home continent, which I could see receding into the haze out the window. Our boss, Dutch, was an easygoing guy. Still, it was a comfort knowing we'd be well beyond the blast radius when he found that expense report.

SHENZHEN, CHINA

Moral Compass Drift

"Shoulder-surfing" for purposes of gathering information while onboard a crowded aircraft should be a high crime or misdemeanor.

The practice of harnessing another passenger's work laptop as your in-flight entertainment is foul business indeed. I don't like it when it happens to me, and I never engage in the practice myself, however tempting.

Almost never.

My excuse, and I'm sticking with it, in this one instance is that I never intended to gather information that way and there was no means for me to unlearn it. We were China bound, and folks in the Boeing 777 cabin were drifting into slumber, as I strolled up the dimly lit aisle to stretch and brush teeth. On a bright laptop screen, my eye caught the logo and company name, "Buddakan Networks." I turned away. Too late.

The owner of this laptop worked for a company I admired. It was well-funded, local, and bound for great things. My own company had recently been acquired. It was no longer the gritty little start-up I'd joined, and in any case, consolidation talk gave me reason to think my days there might well be numbered. The fact that they **weren't** is not more damning; how was I to know that then?

Thus, I schemed up a plan. I knew it bent my own sense of ethics *ever so slightly,* yet I rationalized it this way: I would be taking advantage of *metadata* only. This was shortly after the Ed Snowden affair, and that term was current. Snowden had revealed that the U.S. government had been soaking up information from every telecom trunk line in the years after 911. Not reading or listening into the conversations, no, of course not. Just monitoring the metadata – the "from-tos," the "goes-intos" and the "goes-outtas" – to help protect the homeland from "evil doers."

After arrival in Hong Kong and checking into my hotel, I found my fellow passenger on LinkedIn. The mugshot matched the face I'd seen on my way back from the lav. He was the CEO, on business travel from my same hometown in Northern California, and both of us were headed into Shenzhen. That's where the customers were. Our itineraries would overlap with the largest communications companies in China, who have facilities in that sprawling wild, wild east of the electronics universe.

There were a few job openings on Buddakan's website. I messaged him about one that looked like a fit. I said something like, 'Would love to chat, in China a few days, back next week, can swing by your office then if you've got a few minutes.'

Although nearly midnight in Hong Kong, he responded promptly. "Hey, where in China? I'm in

Shenzhen this week, maybe we can meet for dinner?"

Bingo! The cat was in the bag.

We set a meeting point the next night in the Futian district of Shenzhen. Futian is the focal point for nightlife and revelry, complete with the world's largest restaurant, with seating for thousands in a giant amphitheater. Clubs, discos, sing-along Karaoke palaces (aka KTV) lit-up the night in Futian.

We met at his chosen restaurant and shook hands. We were in the same business and from the same hometown – our kids might be classmates for all we knew – and met now for the first time thousands of miles from home. Ming informed me he was born and raised in Shanghai. He asked: "You're good with authentic Chinese, right?"

"Totally," I said, and then in Chinese: "My wife is from Taiwan." This was kind of a job interview, I thought. Go with the flow, be a team-player, and land the offer.

"Ha!" he laughed. "Your Chinese is not awkward. OK, here we go. So you're really not picky then?"

Oh, no, I communicated. Hell, no. Not me. Truth be told, through my teens I was the pickiest eater on the planet. My childhood mainstays were roast beef, baked potatoes and carrots – raw carrots, not the squishy cooked kind.

That was then, and this was now and the new me. Deft with chopsticks, having survived a year in Taiwan, married to a Chinese woman who cooked, I was a master of exotic cuisines, most particularly Chinese. Chicken feet did not scare me, and delicately sliced pig's ear dipped in vinaigrette? Come on. I'd eaten fried scorpions and the most indelicate organ meats of the ram. By the way, I don't recommend it. The taste glued itself to my tongue for days.

Ming spat out orders to the waitress, who nodded and retreated to the kitchen.

"So, I'll be honest," he said. "We need to bring on new blood quickly, but we're on a cash drip-feed. We'll make room for "A-Game" players only. Tell me what you do." I launched into my elevator pitch, finishing as the first dish arrived.

"You like?" asked Ming, depositing a huge chunk of slimy, cold, tubular grotesqueness on my plate. It resembled neither plant nor beast. "Raw sea cucumber," he affirmed, before stuffing his mouth with a huge globule and chewing it loudly. "Ummm."

Well. Now. I smiled and wielded my chopsticks gamely. I struggled to get a grip on this slippery monstrosity. I gave it the old college try. My food bounced around its plate for an awkward long time.

Like a last minute death row pardon, the Mou Tai arrived. "Oh, wait," said Ming. "Drink first. This is top-drawer, you're going to love it." He sure seemed to know his Mou Tai. He poured the viscous rice wine into our cups. *"Gam bei!"* He threw it back in one gulp. I did the same. Then he squeezed the remainder of the seafaring nightmare blob between his chopsticks, lifted the dripping goo to his mouth, slurped loudly, and made it disappear down the gullet.

"You like?" he repeated. "Oh, here comes the jellyfish."

It, too, was raw, salty, gelatinous and unsightly. Not even 500 million years of evolution had been able to grant this homely creature a single attribute suitable for dining presentation. There was no slicing the grisly toughened medusa with my bamboo tools.

I lifted the entire portion to eye level and scissored away a small bit using my teeth. With a slimy sliver between cheek and gum, traction was lost on the rest of the beast which dropped to the table, missed the plate, and Slinky-ed off the edge into my lap. I feigned an attempt at rescue, but instinct forced my hand – or thigh, anyway – into a wiggle that sent the gelatinous zooplankton to the floor, where it landed with a solid, moist *splat.*

"Well, darn it." I hoped my fake disappointment wasn't too transparent.

Across the table, Ming smiled at my struggle as he chomped away. The waitress's dark ponytail brushed my shoulder as she festooned our table with more dishes. Well, I'd wanted dinner with the CEO, and now I was getting it. Tirelessly, I applied myself to the task of sub-dividing each comestible terror into bits that could be swallowed whole and without mastication. The fried pork intestine was an exception. It at least smelled like something I might want to eat, and had a bit of crunch.

This was a test. I had to display my meddle to have a shot at earning a spot on Ming's team. A stir-fry dish arrived piping hot and sizzling in an iron skillet. Now, *this* I could eat. There was some kind of meat, lots of spicy chiles and whole garlic, even some onion. It wasn't bad at all, and I started to wonder about the meat.

"Good for you!" laughed Ming. "You like the silkworm. Me too. Bottoms up!" The Chinese grain alcohol chased the worm down my throat. I could get through this. I was going to pass the test. Then some kind of steamed veggie arrived, and I made a big show of slurping down as much bitter root as I could, wiping my mouth – with my shirtsleeve, of course, because no traditional Chinese eatery worth its salt ever provides the distraction of a napkin. Yes, I was going to make it.

"Try an egg," suggested Ming, grinning mirthfully. I took one from the bowl that contained four eggs. I had to use my fingers, and was pleased the shell was warm. I cracked it against the table.

"No, no," said Ming. "Watch me." He used his chopstick like a billy club on the top of his egg a few times. Liquid sprayed from it. He tore the top off and poured it into his mouth. "Umm," he intoned, then peeled the shell back further, revealing yellow yoke. And a small bird embryo.

"Baby chicken?" I asked.

"Duck," he said, and extracted the embryo with chopsticks. It was all swollen shut eyes, gaping open tiny beak, and dripping proto-feathers. He made it disappear. Was that the crack of tiny duck bones emanating from his mouth? "Umm," he repeated. "So good."

I sighed. So close to success, I now threw in the towel. There was no possibility of passing this exam. I proceeded to play with my egg, managed to spill out all the liquid, nibbled on the yolk, and proposed yet another toast as delaying action. Ming gobbled down his second egg, which I've since learned is called balut.

"Yumm," he said. "The best. But hey, it's not for everyone. I can eat that other one if you're not into it?"

"By all means, please." While he was busy doing

that, I worked hard to camouflage my one little duck embryo on my plate by hiding it under silkworm and pork intestine remains. "Hiding your food in plain sight," is what my mother used to call me out on. It's a skill I was glad to have retained.

Ming leaned back in his chair and emitted a satisfied belch. "So full. *Xiaojie!*" he yelled at our waitress. She brought him the check, and he waved her very graciously in my direction.

"Weiguoren?" she asked. She meant, *You expect this sadly dyspeptic foreigner to pay your outsize bill? What kind of **monster** are you?*

I might have been imagining that last bit. Like a trooper, I took it. It was impossible to read anything other than the numbers, which exceeded $300 U.S. equivalent. Good thing, I thought, I'm on expense—

Then I remembered: this was supposed to be a job interview. Ethics dictated this was my personal tab. OK, then, so be it. I shelled out the cash. The nightmare was over.

"Let's get a foot massage," said Ming as we hit the sidewalk.

"That sounds great." He was the boss. Maybe. Foot massage is a staple activity in China and is widely available and very inexpensive. Nothing to fear. Until Ming led us into a spa that was lit-up in neon like a Vegas strip casino. We were assisted by nearly toothless older men in stripping down, led to a shower, dried with fluffy towels, and inserted into silk bathrobes. It was all very efficient.

This was the fanciest foot massage palace I'd ever seen, with high ceilings, dramatic red, swooping draperies, and immaculately dressed young men in white tuxedos and the women in low-cut red silk dresses that matched the curtains. Ming was ordering up everything, including fancy cocktails that arrived with little umbrellas.

"After nails," said Ming, "Ear cleaning is next. I build up a lot of wax." We sat side by side in plush chairs with two young women scrubbing our feet in buckets of warm soapy water. Two more walked up and demanded access to our hands. "Manicure," he informed me. "Then pedicure, ears, then wax job. Do you like singing, Tim?"

Dear god, what had I gotten myself into? No shot at a job offer was worth this, and it might not even be a shot. He hadn't shown much interest in what I might do for his company. "Sure," I said, "but I don't want to keep you up late."

"What the hell," he said. "We're traveling. We're tough. No wives or kids. You're not afraid of a late night, are you?"

Yes, I thought. I most certainly am, and thank you for asking. I was jet-lagged, reeling from the Mou Tai, and had a 6:00am alarm already pre-set. Those factors were the least of my worries, though. I now feared for my wallet.

We were in for the full treatment. I wasn't sure what was meant by 'wax' in this instance. The next stop was to be karaoke? Oh, no, I don't think so. I could see this quickly turning into a $4,000 night, and I was beginning to believe that whatever the cost, I alone would bear it. Ming had mentioned his company's cash "drip feed." Oh, dear.

"Late night never bothered me," I found myself lying. "All part of the routine, right?"

Ming's smile grew larger and more animated. It occurred to me I'd just splashed jet-fuel onto the fire.

Then I felt something slide into my left ear.

"OK *ma*?" asked the sweet voice of my ear cleaner.

"OK," I said. It didn't hurt a bit. It felt quite nice, actually, much the way a good haircut proffered by a skilled stylist gently tickles the neck and scalp. Yet this was a deep probing. I found myself wondering about the anatomy of the Eustachian tube; did the right and left ear connect through this avenue? I didn't think so, but now, I wasn't sure. Maybe this cotton swab could safely traverse – in one ear and out the other – and not lobotomize me?

A loud pop and a vibrant giggle signified its withdrawal, followed by the sight of a mountain of yellowish wax that she waved in front of my face for my approval. No question, I was hearing the world at a whole new level. She probed the other ear, all while my fingernails were meticulously and perfectly cut, filed and de-cuticled. Then my toes. Ming had ordered more drinks, and I accepted the straw that was gently fed into my mouth. The drink was fruity and powerful.

There was no way out. The conveyor belt I'd strapped myself to by using accidentally collected metadata – an act that had marginally violated my own standards for ethical business behavior -- now carried me into the waxing. This was, apparently, to be done in a VIP wax room. I saw Ming led away toward his waxy fate before following my own entourage to mine.

The door to the VIP room closed. The lights dimmed. I was instructed by my near-toothless escort to lie down on the "wax couch." I did as instructed, and to my immense relief, he left the room.

The door promptly re-opened and in came a woman who might have been Mrs. Toothless. She was, shall we say, a senior citizen. "Wax," she said, and with that, she began to pull open my bathrobe. Instinct, and the wish that nobody's grandmother should have to look into these nether regions, caused me to restrain the garment.

"No wax?" she asked.

"No wax." Mrs. Toothless waved dismissively and left.

For the next ten minutes, wax-less from the Eustachian tubes on down, I lay dreading what might come through the door next, and how much it would cost. Then it hit me: nobody was coming. Now was the time to get out.

I opened the door, followed the hallway past many other doors, and emerged back into the red-curtained main annex. I found the locker room, showed my wrist bracelet, and was given access to the cage with my street clothes. I started to dress.

"*Bu yau!*" someone shouted. It was Mr. Toothless. "*Hai meiyou!*" Not yet! He re-locked my things, and led me by the arm to the shower room. Ah, yes, cleanliness first. I tossed the robe and scrubbed up under a deluge of spiky lukewarm water.

No sooner had I shut off the tsunami spray, than a soft towel was engulfing my backside as Mr. Toothless dried me. Then he led me, still naked, to a platform. He gestured for me to lie down. As I did so, he erupted in guttural Chinese. Ah, yes. I flipped over onto my stomach. He disappeared from sight, but began whistling. I heard running water filling a bucket.

43

Then I felt the skin of my shoulders being ripped from my bones, so I thought. It ripped back the other direction, then ripped again, and I realized he was using some kind of pumice stone to exfoliate dead skin cells. It seemed for good measure he was stripping off some live cells, too.

While painful, it was invigorating. When he'd finished an area there was a sensation of heat as blood rushed back into the tissues. The process continued down my back. It was both painful and relaxing. I got nervous when he went at my buttocks, but he did not intrude too closely to areas of high sensitivity. Once this process was completed, he helped me stand.

"Neh?" he said, pointing at a considerable pile of dead skin. "Neh? *Neh!*" It was impressive work. He then reversed me back into the shower, dried me again, and escorted me back to my locker. While I dressed, I formulated my fighting retreat. There had to be an escape.

I couldn't very easily run and hide. It was a universal rule, Leave No Man Behind. I decided I would wait for Ming in the lobby. Then I would pay the tab for whatever had been done to us, and inform him of this most critical conference call coming up at 2:00am (it was Monday in the States, after all) that I had totally forgotten. Gotta run, sorry!

As I waited in the lobby, the foolishness of my plan became apparent. First, he'd see right through it. Then, he would tell me to go ahead, step out of the club, do my job, then dive back into the rhythm section, or the conga line, or whatever he was cooking up. No, this plan would not do at all.

It would have to be Plan B. Not great. It would

have the collateral effect of confirming the lie about my love of obscure Chinese cuisine. It might get me off the hook, yet shame would attach. No hope for future redemption. Still, it was that or risk paying a king's ransom for a night of revelry that I neither wanted nor had budgeted.

Presently, Ming appeared, red-faced, white sleeves unbuttoned, hair still wet, smiling, relaxed. "Ready for the next level?"

"Ready as I'll ever be," I said. "Just a little queasy."

"What?" he said. "Well that sucks. Good news, this next place makes a rum and coke that will soothe your tummy. Here, let me grab the bill for you."

Thanks be to heaven, I thought, a financial reprieve! He fired a round of ballistic Chinese at the clerk behind the counter, who proffered a black billfold. Ming pivoted with Kirov ballet grace in my direction. He smiled.

"Here you go," he said, and handed me the invoice for another $500 worth of RMB. I dug deep and came up short.

"Hmm," I said, counting out all the bills in my pocket, save a 50 RMB note for my escape taxi. I was short 40 *kuài*. "I can hit the ATM."

Ming looked annoyed. He turned to the clerk and launched another fusillade of incendiary Mandarin. I thought he might next reach into his back pocket where his own fattened wallet was an indelible protuberance.

"He says we're ok," said Ming. "He's giving us a discount. Hey, did you need this?" Ming waved the receipt at me.

"Not really," I said. "This is my pleasure."

"Oh hey," he said. "Thanks much." Then he folded the receipt, reached back to grab that bulbous wallet full of cash and carefully inserted it.

He *wasn't* going to expense this bill that I'd paid from my own pocket? Was he? Any remaining qualms I'd had about the ethics of engineering a meeting with him now evaporated.

"Oh, hey," he said again. "In that case, can I have the receipt from dinner, too?"

The world seemed to rotate more slowly now. I *was* beginning to feel a bit queasy. I fished out the $300 dinner receipt. "All yours," I said.

"Thanks, buddy. There's an ATM across the street. The club is about 20 minutes by taxi. You good so far?"

No, I'm dying, I thought. I'm spiraling into a yawning pit of despair. I now faced a pocket-money collapse of epic proportions. My final hope was that the ATM would only spit out a few hundred dollars to limit the damages.

"Doing great," I lied. I'd survived the duck embryo, being liberated of all my Chinese currency, and I was determined to protect my sunk costs, and land the job offer.

We walked over to the ATM. I stuck in my bank card, and out came roughly $400 worth of RMB. "Dang, looks like that's my limit."

"Fear not," said Ming. "Try your credit card."

"I don't have a PIN for that one."

"No need," he said. "It's Bank of China. They know you're good for it." He laughed.

Feeling the Earth might now end suddenly, and kind of hoping it would, I stuck my credit card into the ATM. "Try 10,000," he suggested helpfully.

$1500 U.S.

The machine hummed and clunked. It flashed once or twice. Then, to my horror, out surged a mountain of Chinese currency. It seemed to take forever to unspool it all. Please, god, kill me now…

"Gotta take this," said Ming, and he began yakking into his phone. At last the ATM had finished its task. I didn't know where to stick such a wad. I split it into two stacks and jammed both front pockets.

Now there was no choice. Plan B all the way. I would self-induce vomiting. It now seemed attainable. My heart was racing; my head was pounding. I did feel queasy, oh so queasy…

Ming hung up his phone.

I inhaled sharply. "Hey, Ming, I'm sorry—"

"Yeah," he interrupted. "Me too, buddy. So you followed that? Your Chinese *is* good. That's my customer, they want to party now. It's strictly a locals only scene, you know what I mean?"

What? What was this? I thought.

"Oh, gosh," I said. "Totally. I *completely* understand."

"Cool, hey thanks, buddy. Let's catch up tomorrow, do this again, and hit the KTV?"

"Oh, yeah, maybe." I was cool. I suppressed the joy swelling within, tried to keep it off my face. "Yeah, let's play it by ear and text tomorrow."

"OK, man, good sport!" He flagged a cab. "Know your way back?"

"Sure do!"

He jumped into the cab. "Thanks for dinner! Talk to you tomorrow." And off he went.

I was free. Bloodied but unbowed. On the

wrong side of $800, and on the wrong side of my own ethical standards, yet I had survived. I flagged my own cab. On the ride back to the hotel, my pants pockets stuffed with cash, just one little thing troubled me:

Strictly a locals thing? Strictly a *locals* thing?

Well, dammit, man, how can *he* be a local and *not me* when we live in the *same damn town!*

YANGTZE RIVER BASIN, CHINA

Export Restrictions

Most visitors to China see the coast. On this trip, I was excited to see some of what China is made of, on the inside. Of all the very famous Chinese cities, only a few are in the interior – Xian, Chengdu, Chongqing, Wuhan, Kunming – and these are more representative of their coastal brethren than of the vast Chinese provincial interior.

Another way to view it: there are over 100 cities in China with a population of one million or more people. Of these, more than 80% are within 100 miles of the Pacific Ocean. On previous trips, I'd gone "deep" inside only a few times.

Gary and I drove onward, albeit slowly, from Nanjing up the Yangtze River Valley, deeper into the Chinese hinterlands. Every few minutes we would pass a "town" parked on either side of the kilometer-wide band of water. Many of these were home to half a million people. But mostly, I noticed, we passed a multitude of huge powerplants with the characteristic tall tapering tower one sees adjacent to most nuclear power stations.

"Coal?" I asked Gary.

"Yes. Most of China's power still comes from coal. But see, many are not operating." True, smoke issued from just a handful of the dozens and dozens we'd passed. "The government wants to go green. Quickly."

We'd driven much of the day and were now deep into what many call "the provinces."

This term refers to the vast majority of China, which is comprised of 38 provinces and some special territories. But the places most foreigners visit – Beijing, Shanghai, Shenzhen – are nothing like the provinces. The term, nearly pejorative, is best translated into English as "the Back 40." Or maybe "Flyover country."

We were halfway from Nanjing to Hefei, the capital city of China's answer to Arkansas. With no offense intended to either Arkansas or Anhui -- both of which I can attest are filled with friendly people who love their homeland -- in their respective nations, these states share a commonality in being perceived as among the most culturally remote regions.

It was there in a small city on the south bank of the river that Gary and I arrived to meet a curious customer. Curious for their remote location. Curiouser for their behavior.

Two men greeted us and led us to a conference room. The procurement director, who sported a short buzz cut, was clearly in charge. The other, whose card said "CTO," looked like he wanted to be somewhere else.

"We want," said the director, "to use your sensor in our VacuBot 9000. If you can meet our expectations." The VacuBot prototype sat on the table beside the CTO. It looked to be a robotic vacuum cleaner, an iRobot Roomba wannabe.

"Our VacuBot is much smarter than Roomba," the procurement officer informed us. "Do you know why?"

Hazarding a guess was, well, hazardous. A correct answer could spook the customer and create unproductive tension. A well-educated incorrect answer might also go awry, as the customer might begin to wonder if we had just given away some other company's secret sauce. This was not my first Roomba knock-off visit, and I was ready. "Perhaps it's due to excellent engineering? And, of course, with our sensors, you'll have top-of-the-line mapping and tilt."

"Roomba has all that, too." He raised his chin, which I took as a challenge to confirm or deny this assertion.

I shrugged. "I can't rightly say."

"You know," said the buzz cut boss, "but won't tell us." The CTO sat upright in his chair at this. He smiled at us. I sensed his embarrassment.

"Of course," I said, "*if* I know, I can't tell you. So you can be sure we don't compromise our customer's valuable concepts to competitors."

"Humph!" he said. Like most Chinese customers, this state of affairs appeared adequate but not sufficient. Some would make no bones about it, asking multiple questions about their competitors while swearing us up-and-down to never whisper a word of their own activities. Which we never would.

"OK," the director said. "This I can tell you: our robot has a denser constellation of sensors than any other. We use gyro, accelerometer, magnetometer with tilt and direction feeds. We have GPS, derived from a proprietary source."

Of course, he must have been talking about the 3G wireless network. Many consumer systems were now designed to "poach" their geolocation – literally, their position on the Earth's sphere, to within a few meters accuracy. "Very impressive," I said.

"There's more. Our algorithms were written by top experts in Dead Reckoning from Fudan University," the Chinese equivalent of Oxford or MIT. The use of DR technology in a simple household vacuum robot, if true, struck me as overkill.

And unlikely, given its expense to develop and its complexity. Our company's top mathematician had described it like this: "Usable DR is still a pipedream. It's a mathematical trail of bread crumbs left in the wake of a cyclone. In theory, it can be done. It'll work for a few turns, then the math just explodes."

Dead Reckoning attempts to isolate exact position from calculating the results of all motion vectors generated by all accelerations – up, down, back, forth, side-to-side – over a given time. Marginally effective in the age of three-masted sloops, remarkably executed by Charles Lindbergh on the first trans-Atlantic flight, it would be expensive and ineffective excess for an appliance whose job it was to scoop up cat fur and cookie dust.

Maybe "The VacuBot 9000 – Now with Dead Reckoning!" would appear on store shelves as marketing hype.

"You know," said the purchasing officer, "the China market is very large. And our products also target Europe, Japan, Korea, and the U.S.A. In China alone, the total available market is 100 million units per year."

What was coming next was very familiar. Talkative procurement officers always give bloated forecast estimates in an effort to get the vendor salivating, and set him or her up for deep discounting.

"That's big," I said. "Maybe your competition will take some?"

"No," he dismissed my objection out of hand. "VacuBot is the leader. We are first to market with best features. And best price." He tapped his pen on the desk and locked eyes with me.

"We can scale to meet your demand," I said.

"What is your 100 million piece price?" he asked.

"We can work something up for you, certainly. Quantity breaks from 100 to 100,000 pieces. You can draw a curve from there with confidence out to any annual quantity you like. Meantime, perhaps we can review your design requirements."

"You won't give me the 100 million price today?" he asked.

"Will you *buy* 100 million pieces today?"

He laughed. "We also work with *your* competitor." Then he fished out something from a folder on the table in front of him. A blotchy copy of a product datasheet. It had our logo on it.

I applied my best poker face. "What's that?" I asked, knowing damn well what it was.

"We need your MX-007."

This product didn't exist, not here, at least. We'd designed it with grant money from a U.S. government agency, an office within the Department of Defense that funded promising technologies. It was intended for DoD approved customers only. I tried not to string them along. "We can't offer such a product, but if we could, it would be too expensive for the VacuBot market."

The boss bit his lip. "Different project," he conceded. "I can't tell you any details. But we need your MX-007."

He tossed the sheet on the table in front of me. It was a very smudgy copy of a copy of a copy. I surmised he wasn't the only guy in China who had this. When I glanced up to catch his eye, his face was broadcasting "gotcha now."

"This is not generally available," I informed him.

"Don't lie to me," he said.

"Where did you get this?" I asked, just so I didn't have to address his assertion of dishonesty.

"We have sources," he said with a smile. "We know you have this product."

The U.S. Army used this product as battlefield back-up to GPS failure or jamming. It could help put an object exactly where intended from miles away. There was a good reason we didn't sell this product to anyone else.

This was Gary's customer, too. I glanced at him to see if he wanted to field any of this. But he was looking down at the table. At the MX-007 datasheet and specs. He couldn't help himself. Et tu, Gary? As I reached across to grab the sheet, he glanced up at me, a look of pain on his face.

"So," I said. "We don't have such a product available. For export. Right now."

The CTO looked even more pained than Gary, rubbing his eyes, face in hand.

"Why do you think I would believe you?" The boss's tone was now menacing. Suddenly, this meeting now felt like a crazy outta-control toboggan ride – straight downhill.

******

My mind flashed back to a story a co-worker, Terry, had told me. He'd visited one of the most important communications gear makers in China to fix a problem. He'd walked into the customer's facility in Shenzhen on Monday morning. He hadn't walked out again until Saturday night. He meant to, but the customer insisted he stay. Right there. In the lab. Working the issue, with the customer's engineering team. They fed him, and they let him sleep, in a bunk bed in a dormitory room on the floors above the lab. With some very nice roommates. The food was good. When he'd explained that he needed to get his clothes from the hotel, they sent people to take care of that for him.

They held him hostage until the issue was fixed. He couldn't even excuse himself for "comfort breaks" without employee accompaniment. At one point his designated escort was a young woman who'd tried to follow Terry into the men's room.

Terry had had to draw the line, so to speak. She'd reluctantly waited outside the men's room door, frequently knocking. "Like every 15 seconds," Terry recounted. "It was crazy. I joked about them giving me striped pajamas or an orange jumpsuit. They didn't get that at all."

Captive for nearly a week, the customer finally approved the lab results, and let Terry "go free." They even took him to a nice banquet to celebrate. "The irony," he'd told me, "was that the problem wasn't us, but *their* design. Their spec didn't match ours. I wasn't one to harp, cause then they'd start shopping the competition. The engineers knew this was all wrong. They were embarrassed as hell, and really nice to me." Terry had kept his cool. "I told their boss how great they were to work with. And live with. Plus, hey, they'd given me the top bunk."

******

That story had been funny – at the time. Now, I was seriously considering my escape options. I could see the CTO's discomfort grow; maybe he knew what his counterpart had in store for us?

"So tell you what," I told the boss, "If you don't mind me taking this for reference," and I jammed the blotchy MX-007 datasheet into my backpack, and stood up, signaling we were all done here, "I can confer with our team about the possibility of actually building something like this. For export. For you guys."

Gary was on his feet, mumbling, pointing at his watch. I surmised he was making polite excuses about how late we were for the next meeting.

The procurement boss was hesitating and giving me the *look*. "Not so fast," he said. He ran his hand over the top of his buzz cut. He looked at me, then at Gary. Then he turned to glare at his CTO, who shook his head in a gesture I interpreted as, "don't look at me, buddy, you're on your own."

At last, the procurement officer sighed. "OK," he said. "You can go now. Take the sheet. We have copies, of course."

"Of course," I said.

"You will check with your team?" he asked.

"Absolutely," I said. "Our job is to help customers."

The boss came around the table, and approached me. We locked eyes. His were bright, plaintive. "And," he said. "I hope you will not discuss this with anyone else."

"We maintain a wall around each customer's proprietary information," I assured him.

"That's good. I don't want to have a visit from your CIA." He smiled.

I laughed. "It's a long drive to get here," I joked. "So I think that's unlikely."

We shook hands and made our escape. Outside, Gary mumbled, "let's get the hell out of here," and drove with uncharacteristic speed for the next three hours on the highway along the banks of the Yangtze.

It was quiet for a long time, until he suddenly blurted out, "They should not put Dead Reckoning into the vacuum cleaner! What are they thinking?"

"It answers the question," I said. "China, despite labels to the contrary, has gone capitalism crazy. Putting military R&D into a consumer product is good old-fashioned Yankee ingenuity." Gary had nothing to say to that. He leaned harder on the accelerator.

We arrived in Nanjing and passed a quiet evening at the Han Ting Inn – China's answer to the Motel6 – happy in the knowledge that tomorrow night we'd be back in Shanghai. And civilization.

SHANGHAI

Defenestration

Trapped like a rat, I now realized. Appropriate, given my Chinese zodiac sign.

It was unclear what my options were now. None looked good. How did I manage to dip myself into this vat of troubles? Worse, it wasn't the first time. I ought to have known better.

"Sit down," she said. "You can't stand up."

On that count, she was completely wrong, and she'd triggered my memory of the last line of the book "Johnny Tremain."

"Yes, I can. Did you know that sitting is considered the new smoking?"

From her reclined position on the faux leather sofa, she attempted to wave me down. "Don't you know it's very rude in China to stand when you're invited to sit."

"That's interesting" I said. "It's also rude to over-charge your customers. Anywhere."

The woman, who owned this little establishment, was not cowed. "You ordered a drink, and now you don't want to pay for it. I'm very polite. I have not yet called the police."

"I choose to pay a fair market price," I reminded her. It was a single Tsingtao beer, untouched, still in the slightly smudged glass that her daughter or niece, Ling-Ling, had poured it into. Ling-Ling was twenty-something, and a good salesperson. As I'd walked by this pub, she had beseeched me to have a drink.

"Our bar is very comfortable," she'd said with a coquettish smile, "and our business is so small now. Won't you please?" My evening stroll through Shanghai – a city of over 25 million people – had sparked thirst. I'd seen no harm in having a quick quaff, and had followed her into the confines of the intimate pub.

I'd watched her pour the frothy beer into a slightly smudged glass. Despite my parched throat, when she'd asked, "OK to buy me a drink, too?" I'd had the presence of mind to tap the brakes on the proceedings.

"How much for the beer?" I'd asked.

"Let me check," she'd said, getting up to fetch a drink menu. I knew instantly what game this was. But too late. The absence of any other customer in the tiny bar completed the picture.

Ling-Ling returned with the drink menu, the proprietress in tow. Instead of handing it me to me, she pushed, "I'd like a lady's drink. Is that ok?"

"How much is the beer?" I repeated.

"Just one ladies drink, please."

"You can't drink alone," said the boss. "Please, buy her one drink."

That's when I stood up. "Don't worry, I'm not drinking alone."

"But you've ordered beer," the boss said, and behind her in the narrow hallway a large shadow now loomed. A man, and I mean a really big guy, took a step into the room. I assessed he would represent something of an immovable object to me should I make a break for the front door.

"What do you charge for a beer?" I reasserted.

The boss made a show of her displeasure, but she was ready. "If you don't want to be social, then you can pay up now and leave." She dropped a billfold which landed with a loud "slap" on the table. I bent to pick it up, and at the same time caught peripheral sight of Ling-Ling making her escape. The big man barely let her squeeze by. He wasn't taking any chances.

Scrawled on the single sheet of paper: "6,000 RMB." The equivalent at that time of $900 U.S. dollars.

I gave the boss a look, to which she responded: "You didn't order a ladies drink. Ladies drink is only 100 RMB, plus gives 50% discount to the tab. That would be only $3,100 RMB. Now too late."

"May I take a look at the menu?"

The boss handed it over. I flipped through it, confirming my suspicion. There were drinks, but not one had a price. "May I see the menu with the $900 beer?"

"Seasonal pricing," she said, then laughed.

"I'll pay you $100 RMB," I informed her. About $15.00. Over-generous, but did I mention that the bouncer was really, really big? "That's my best offer."

"Ha!" she scoffed. "That's what you Americans do, isn't it? You tell other people what's what, and they must accept it."

While I had to score her a point in the geopolitical sense for that comment, it did nothing but harden my resolve. "Well spoken," I said. "Americans should be more flexible. So, in that spirit, I've changed my mind. I'll pay you 50 RMB. Any other bar in Shanghai, I can get a Tsingtao in a dirty glass for half that. It's a good offer. You should take it."

She laughed again and flung herself onto the sofa facing me. "Please, sit." The stand-off was in full swing. "You must sit." I smiled, and assumed as rigid a stance as I could. The better to increase the awkwardness of the situation. She crossed her legs left, then right. "Sit down, please."

"I prefer to stand."

"You're being rude," she said.

"I'm American," I reminded her. "It's what we do."

"Ha! You can stand there all night, I don't care."

"Thanks," I said. "Very kind of you."

With concerted effort, I maintained eye contact. The more she grimaced at me, the harder I tried to broaden my smile. It had to be creepy for her. It was, frankly, even giving me the willies. Enough of that, I decided to break the tension.

"I need to use the restroom," I said. "Do you mind?"

She looked flummoxed, maybe a little relieved. "No, of course not." She gave orders in Shanghainese, and the very large guy stepped forward. He tried to take my arm, but I gently declined. Then he gestured the way. I thanked him, and locked the door.

Squat toilet, tiny wash basin, no towels or toilet paper. At least all this was normal, and there was a measure of comfort in that. I assessed the bathroom window. It was high up, and very small. Not a complete disappointment, since I didn't really want to instigate a manhunt and an international incident by re-enacting "The Great Escape."

I reflected. Yes, this was stupid. Doubly so, as I'd been here once before...

It was Dale's 30th birthday, and we were cleaning up at the blackjack tables at the Tropicana in Las Vegas. All four of us loved 21, but hey, your buddy only turns 30 once, and besides, he was likely to be engaged soon. We simply had to do something special, something edgy, something more than watching an NFL game together and eating Cheetos. As science fiction geeks, we'd hardly done that a few times. Something special was mandatory.

We'd seen a neon-lit "gentleman's club" next door, and after a steak dinner, we dragged poor Dale there. I don't think any of us were that enthusiastic. We were greeted by an attractive blond woman wearing a tight-fitting black leotard, and she led us to the bar. That was the last we saw of her.

The bartender wore dark slacks, white dress shirt with rolled-up long sleeves, and was conspicuously missing an important lower incisor. "Whatcha havin'?"

We ordered four bottles of Corona, with a lime twist. There was no further preamble; no sooner had the caps come off the bottles, he pushed a billfold at me. "Cash only, in advance."

As the tab read $400, it was good that nobody had had a chance to touch their beer.

"Ooh," I said, "Sorry. Didn't realize this was a

VIP spot."

The bartender had put his elbow on the polished wood bar, and leaned in, narrowing the distance from my nose to his steely black-eyed gaze to just a few centimeters. "Pay up now, punk." His breath was most unpleasant, and I recollect he demonstrated none of the expected self-consciousness regarding the bits of spittle that flew at speed from his mouth onto my face.

"You don't want to deal with Las Vegas's finest," he said. "They know how to handle types like you, and it ain't pretty."

I leaned away, and wiped the spittle with my sleeve. "What the hell," I said. "What do you mean 'types'?" People who know me tend to think I'm generally pleasant. But people who *really* know me have witnessed my hair-trigger temper. I was feeling very triggered.

"Defenestrators," he intoned. "If I call the cops," and he lifted a black desktop phone off its cradle to underscore his point, "they will arrest you all for defenestration."

Roger sprung to my defense, sort of. "Do you even know what that word means?" he asked. I turned to give him a "pipe-down" gesture, but Roger – a top-flight English student who also knew some French and German – continued: "I'm pretty sure you have no idea. Defenestration is the act of knocking someone out a window. I think." That's when I noticed the three immense gentlemen now standing a few feet behind us. So, this was how it was going to be.

The bartender sneered. "Here's another word you pukes might recognize better," he said. He followed up not with *one* word we recognized better, but a string of colorful descriptors that – in fairness – was pretty darn impressive. I almost forgot he was insulting us in a way that demeaned our masculinity and implied we would be found as attractive dates for the balance of the evening by others locked up in the Las Vegas jail.

"That's all you'll be by about midnight in that jail cell. Unless you do the citizenly thing, and pay your *fucking* bill."

And here, I'd like to relay a story of defiance, of grand valor, of wimpy, geeky but intellectually superior blackjack players who banded together in phalanx to gain the upper hand on the evil bullies, bullies who threw around $50 words they didn't dimly understand. Yeah, that would, indeed, be a great story.

But that's not quite the way it went down.

Our attempts to negotiate a more reasonable extortion fee merely turned up the level of threats and pugilistic invective (score me $50 on each of *those* two words, if you don't mind).

After a few minutes of these insults, our resolve collapsed. We paid up, and left quickly, tails sheepishly between our legs. We went back to our shared hotel room, bellyached for a few minutes, then returned to the blackjack tables to drink a few free beers and drown our sorrows and shame in card play.

In Shanghai, alone with the odds stacked against me, I resolved that history was *not* going to repeat. In the tiny bar's one and only restroom, with the gentle giant tapping on the door to make sure I was still captive, I put my credit cards and most of my cash between my sock and my shoe. Then I emerged.

"Better?" said the boss, still reclining on her faux leather sofa.

"Much," I replied politely, resuming my stand-off position.

"Please, sit,"

"I don't think so," I told her.

She shrugged and flipped open her phone. "Hi baby," she said in English. "I have one of your countrymen here. He won't pay his bill and won't sit down." So, her boyfriend was American. She prattled on about something, then put the phone to her shoulder and asked me, "Would you like to talk to my honey?"

"Nope," I said.

She put the phone back to her ear. "He doesn't want to talk to you." She listened, her face squinting. "No, he's not causing trouble. Just refuses to sit down. And says he'll only pay 100 *kuai*."

"Fifty," I reminded her. "I'm now at fifty, going lower soon."

She squinted, held up a finger indicating that I was to pipe down. She nodded. "OK, baby. I'll try." She closed the phone.

"My boyfriend is from Boston. He says he'll give you the lady drink discount after all. Fifty percent off."

"I don't want it," I said. "I note the absence of any ladies. And the Red Socks can suck it."

"You have a bad attitude," she said.

"I'm the customer. *My* attitude is not at issue. *Yours* is." I said it, and was briefly impressed by my ability to be an absolute asshole.

Now she was genuinely uncomfortable. "How much will you pay?"

"I told you. Fifty *kuai*," I said. "Although that glass is dirty."

She laughed. "You'll be here a long time."

"So will you," I said. "So will he." I pointed to her enforcer. "I don't see any other customers, but in the unlikely event that any should come through that door, I'll warn them immediately about your high prices and hardball tactics. And, the dirty glassware."

"Look," she said. "We're not here to make trouble for you, but you *must* pay your bill."

"I agree," I said. I pulled out all the money that was still in my pocket. Then I turned the pocket inside out, did the same with the other. I slapped my back pockets. "That's all I've got. Can you make change?"

She stood and grabbed the 100 RMB note. She looked at it, then up at me. Her face was now contorted. It's possible I'm mistaken, but I do believe that I've never before or since observed such a look of toxic despicability.

"That's ok," I said. "Keep the change."

"Get *out* of here!" she screamed, pointing a very red, dangerously long fingernail just under my nose.

"Get *out!* "

The very last time I'd heard such a commandment issuing from an alpha female, it was my mother's voice, right after she'd accidentally discovered the dead mouse I'd planted floating in a bowl of milk and cereal intended for my younger brother.

Instinct dictated obedience. This time, I did as ordered. I had to squeeze by the bouncer, who to my surprise whispered "thank you," in Chinese; probably just habit. I pushed on the door and it swung open, but before I left to breathe the cool evening air and freedom, I turned and said, "The extra fifty is a tip, for Ling-Ling. Please make sure she gets it."

Then, I did something I rarely do, and never do well. I ran.

The streets of the Maoming district of Shanghai were quiet, so I could hear if they followed me. I wanted to be as far as possible from that place before the boss or her boyfriend or the bouncer caught on to what a slow moving fool I was, and chased me down.

I dove into a thin, dark alley on my right. I ran the length of its narrow, drying-laundry-strewn length and pivoted left into another alley. I jumped like an Olympic hurdler over a fat, white napping cat then dodged right, left, then right again.

There were no sounds of pursuit. I had made my escape. I was happily lost in a deep network of residential alleys, and had no idea where to go. After catching my breath, playing with my compass, and asking a few kindly elders sitting on their porch to soak up the evening air, I eventually found a pathway back to the Huang-Pu River. There was a major street, then a waiting taxi.

For the second time in my life, I'd evaded the crime of defenestration. I still don't know what this is, but by god I'm hell-bent **not** to be caught doing it a third time.

TRADERS

SHINJUKU, TOKYO

The Peddlers

"Very good, Floyd-san," said Ozawa. "I very like this product." He held it high above the gleaming table in one of his company's conference rooms on forty-second floor of a new office skyscraper. His eyes sparkled, from our view across the table, against a dazzling Tokyo cityscape that stretched away as far as vision would take it this overcast summer day.

Again, Floyd pushed the little red button on the RF controller in his hand, and Ozawa chuckled as the little chopper whirred for a second time around the conference room, before Floyd brought it to a not-so-gentle landing on the polished wood-top between us.

Floyd was a genius salesman. He always had a demo for any product he peddled. And I do mean *always*.

I felt something hit my shoe under the table. That would be Floyd, right on time. I turned to him and winked. Below his neat "silver-fox" gray cut, Floyd's face wore that happy "told you so" grimace he'd given me several times this week. Just before meeting Ozawa, he'd boasted in the elevator.

"Ozawa-san knows value, he knows consumer trends, and I know Ozawa-san. I've worked with him for 20 years."

"You guys go way back," I affirmed.

"Yes," said Floyd, "but it's more than that. Ozawa-san and I, we are, how do you say in Japanese...muy sympatico." I laughed at that.

"We're going to show him some products," said Floyd. "He's going to love them all, and he's going to place at least trial orders for all of them. You watch."

The elevator doors opened as he finished and at that same moment I remembered our beer and peanut talk of the previous night. This was *the* Ozawa-san. This was indeed a special customer.

The previous evening over chilled glasses of Asahi, Floyd had briefed me on the next day's customer meetings, as was his routine each night of this week-long "campaign" in Japan. He'd tallied up the morning meetings, quaffed his beer, and ordered our customary second round. "In the afternoon we'll meet Ozawa and Fuji Bank, both in Shinjuku."

"What's Ozawa?" Floyd had then explained that Ozawa was a long-time friend who ran a consumer products distribution company, with powerful channels into Sogo and the other major and chic department stores of Japan. If he bought something, it was always a big deal. Usually, he bought everything Floyd recommended.

"Which is why I choose my products for Ozawa-san very, very carefully. Our relationship is too important to risk discord by peddling a product that doesn't fit."

Floyd had then explained that on the second of

September 1944, as a newly-minted ensign in the U.S. Navy, he had stood in full dress uniform along with the crew of the U.S.S. Missouri in Tokyo Bay. He'd witnessed the surrender of the Japanese Empire, the end of World War II. He had seen Douglas MacArthur accept the formal end of hostilities from the Emperor's representative.

"It was a moment I'll never forget," he'd said. "It's the moment that hooked me on Japan, and why I now choose to spend the sunset years of my long business career in the land of the Rising Sun."

Then he'd mentioned that Ozawa-san had been there, too. "He was like me. We both had just been inducted into our respective navies. Lucky for us both we arrived too late to see action. When we first sat down to a business dinner together 30 years later, we had no idea we'd both been floating in Tokyo Bay that morning. Saké has a way of ensuring full disclosure, and when we discovered this amazing coincidence late that evening, it was as if we were long separated twins. Blood brothers. We've been in business ever since."

"What else have you got?" asked Ozawa-san, rubbing his hands together. I think he enjoyed these product rollout sessions with Floyd, and no doubt looked forward to saying "yes" to a deal with his old friend.

That was my cue. I reached into my over-sized backpack and pulled out the demo kit for our third and final product of the day, which Floyd had neatly packaged in an artisan wood case with metal clamps. It was about the size of a small milk carton. I pushed it across the table to Floyd.

"This," he said with Shakespearean flair as he clicked open the shiny silver clamps. "This is something you'll really appreciate, as will your environmentally-minded customers."

Ozawa-san grunted in satisfaction. "We need more products to save our Earth," he affirmed.

The box contained a small bottle with a blue and white label featuring silvery bubbles. A cleaning product. The label read, "Nitro-Scrub." On either side of the bottle were two small saké glasses. Floyd removed all three objects and placed them reverently on the table. Then he stood, held the bottle with both hands, and began his pitch.

"You see, Ozawa-san, you enjoy life in a nation that values cleanliness."

"Hai!" said Ozawa.

"Throughout Japan, I admire the streets free of litter, finely starched clothing and pressed uniforms of workers and students, the pride of the people expressed in their beautiful flower arrangements and meticulously clean homes and businesses."

"Honto!" said Ozawa – true! – leaning back in his chair, fingers stitched together on his immaculate white shirt over his stomach. His satisfied smile grew larger.

"The Japanese people also take to heart the cleanliness, not just of their own personal homes, but the shared home that is their nation, as well as the shared community provided by our precious planet."

"Hai!"

Floyd began pacing the room behind me. I discretely slid my chair to one side to make a clear view of the "stage" for Ozawa-san.

"Modern science marches forward in all

directions," said Floyd, "and new technologies for easier and more efficient cleaning, while at the same time protecting our planet, are coming to market all the time. Nitro-Scrub is the latest product of chemical engineering advancements in this regard."

"Ooooo…" said Ozawa-san.

"Nitro-Scrub is new, patented, and utterly unique in the household cleaning product category." Floyd then impressed us both with a quick recitation of both the Japanese and global total available markets for household cleaning fluids that fell into the environmentally friendly segment. It was a very large number of billions of yen per year. It felt gratuitous, because I sensed Ozawa was already sold.

"Nitro-Scrub goes down the drain with waste-water, and unlike other products, when it gets to the oceans, it harmlessly decomposes over hours into safe natural constituents – oxygen, nitrogen, and trace amounts of chlorides."

"Hai," said Ozawa. "Very natural."

"Indeed," said Floyd, "so natural that it harms no fish, plankton, or marine mammals. It's a wonder of modern cleansing technology that meets the needs of busy homemakers and keeps our planet green and safe for all."

"Honto!" said Ozawa.

"Honto!" said Floyd, and with a dramatic turn, placed his right hand on the bottle cap, and cranked it open. With no hesitation, he poured an ounce or so of the clear liquid into each of the two sake cups. He capped the bottle, put it down, and deftly slid one of the cups to me. He picked up the other.

I knew what to do. I stood. I picked up the cup. I held it with both hands as Floyd was doing.

Like Floyd, I turned to Ozawa and gave a small bow. Then, we both turned back to each other.

"Kan pei!" said Floyd.

"Kan pei!" I repeated.

"Ooooo…." said Ozawa.

I did as Floyd did. This was sales mentoring second to none. I would follow my fearless leader anywhere.

Floyd lifted the cup to his lips, his eyes locked with mine. I did the same. His right eye twitched. He tilted his glass, as I did with mine. Liquid entered my mouth. It exerted a pungent, active chemical sensation on my tongue. It was nothing bad, but very different. I could feel it going to work on my mouth as Scope would, but without the minty freshness.

Floyd lowered his cup, smacked his lips lustily, and set it down. "So you see…" he said.

I followed suit, except I didn't say anything. I had Nitro-Scrub in my mouth. I swallowed it.

Some kind of wave traveled up my throat. Like a ping pong ball squeezing its way up past a series of baffles: "*gr-dug gr-dug gr-dug gr-dug gr-dug gr-dug gr-dur gr-dug*," but it was quiet. Then, something arrived at my trachea – it hit me: an overwhelming urge to hack up both lungs. I felt my chest constrict, my ears turning crimson.

Little stray lights began to circle in the conference room, though I think only *I* could see them, and they spun faster and faster as if being sucked into a quasi-dimensional vortex. Somehow, I battled it back, almost. Then, I surrendered to the unstoppable force of nature. Covering my mouth, it opened, and out emerged a single, light cough.

That was met with a quick, stern glance from

Floyd. I put the cup down and sat.

Ozawa-san was on his feet. "Floyd-san, Tim-san, I love this product. When can you deliver 10,000 cases?"

"Er," said Floyd, "cases? You mean bottles?"

"Twelve bottles per case, like standard? I want 10,000 cases."

Floyd beamed. "Well," he opened his little notepad. "Standard lead time is six weeks, but let us get back to you with an expedited delivery schedule, if we may."

Ozawa-san was beaming. "Yes, of course, Floyd-san." We were *all* beaming.

I beamed despite the trail of flames that had lit up my esophagus like it was the Hindenburg on final approach. Imagine you've just taken a swig from a very hot cup of coffee into which someone had squirted petroleum jelly laced with eucalyptus and freshly squeezed bee venom. Tears welled in my eyes, my breathing was accelerated and I felt my heart skip a few beats as it tried to calibrate what had just happened here.

"So sorry," said Ozawa-san, "I have a new meeting."

"We are your humble servants," said Floyd. We stood and packed everything away. A smiling Ozawa led us to the elevator. We shook hands.

"I'm sorry," he said. "Tim-san, you are not feeling well?"

Floyd stepped in, which was great, because I couldn't speak. My throat was in open revolt. I grinned and wiped tears before they ran too far down my face.

"Tim-san hasn't felt too good since dinner last

night," Floyd lied. "He thinks his sashimi might have been exposed to Fugu puffer fish. I told him, nonsense, you're still alive!"

We all laughed. Well, those two laughed. I just kept beaming and hoped for a swift and painless death once outside Ozawa's office. I did not wish to die in front of Ozawa and incur the wrath of my mentor for having blown the deal.

I jabbed the down button on the elevator panel. My one strongest anecdotal data point for the existence of a benign super being is that, within seconds, the elevator doors opened. We hastily stepped in, bowed very low, and were rewarded with the doors closing on a smiling, waving, bowing Ozawa-san.

"You know it won't kill you," said Floyd.

Blessed liberation. I leaned forward into the corner of the elevator car, and hacked. It was an awful sound, even to me. The convulsion lasted most of the journey down to lobby level, and as the elevator slowed, I straightened up and looked at my covering hand. To my surprise, no blood was evident.

Regarding phlegm, let's just say it was minimal given the violence my pulmonary system had just endured. Floyd reached into his bag and gave me a hotel water bottle which I emptied in seconds as we stepped into the lobby.

We stood momentarily there, me leaning against the wall, catching my breath. "That was amazing, Floyd."

"I'm pleased," he said. "You're a good understudy, though you misread my wink."

"Wink? I thought you had a speck in your eye."

"Not to fluster," he said. "Although," he reached into my bag and riffled out the bottle of Nitro-Scrub, "I am wondering exactly what is in this crap." He read the ingredients. "Nope. Yep." He gazed at me, a nervous look on his face. "Nope. We're good. No need for hospitalization. Just don't get any in your eyes."

And off we went to peddle our wares to Fuji Bank.

TIM JENKINS

LOS ANGELES

Honey

Michael was a freelance businessman, a "gun-slinger." He had brought us a number of deals, matched us with an electronic point-of-sale company, linked us to commodity trades and U.S. suppliers for some big proposals out of China that our Beijing team urgently wanted us to broker.

Having established his credibility, Michael – a Chinese American – walked in one morning dressed in his usual gray suit and too-thin black tie. I was starting to think that was all he had to wear. He hadn't come alone, but with a far better dressed female attaché.

"This is Honey. She only speaks Chinese." I shook her hand and met her eyes. She had a Hollywood smile and was made up and dressed like a starlet. She wore deep blue lipstick, rouge, thick black hair stylishly coiffed, and a fashionable blue beret set at a jaunty angle. She looked a little nervous to me.

"Where's Mr. Sheng?" asked Michael. "He's expecting us."

I led them to the company's "big room" which

contained an oak table sized for a dozen. I knocked on the double doors and, hearing a grunt from beyond, entered.

Mr. Sheng was playing with a marker pen and glaring at the wall-to-wall white board on which he'd scrawled a number of business problems. While they were all written in Chinese, I recognized the deals: electronic point of sale system, juice and sugar trade, and a dozen more.

"Sheng *xiān sheng*," I announced, "Your visitors are here."

He turned with a smile and came to shake Michael's hand. Then he looked at Honey and said "Wahhh." He said that a lot. It's Chinese for "wow," but far more versatile. He gestured graciously and they pulled up chairs. I started for the door.

"You should stay for this one," said Michael. "Wouldn't you agree, Mr. Sheng?" My boss nodded, so I found a chair across from Michael.

He launched into his pitch, as he always did, in fast Chinese. His Chinese was not very good, if I may be so bold. I don't speak much, but I know what proper Mandarin sounds like and native speakers have told me I replicate that well. Michael's Mandarin was *mǎ mǎ hǔ hǔ* as the Chinese say – horse horse tiger tiger, meaning 'so-so.' No surprise, he was born in Hong Kong and his native tongue was Cantonese.

Mr. Sheng could understand him well enough. Or almost well enough.

"Sorry," Mr. Sheng interrupted in English. "Sorry, what's that?"

Michael halted, flustered. He flicked his gaze to me and blinked. Honey sat next to him, apparently fascinated by the tabletop. Michael re-wound and started again, in English. "OK, we covered this on the phone, but…" then he launched into bar-brawl Chinese again.

When I can't follow a business conversation in Chinese, I watch body language. I have some facility in this, too. I'm better at transmission, as people can read me like a book, which is why I don't play poker. I can read the room, and I could follow Michael's gestures and posture, which communicated annoyance. Mr. Sheng's eye were lit in wonderment, his face quizzical. This was his "WTF" face that I knew well. Honey was somewhere between bored and nervous.

"Uh," interrupted Mr. Sheng, holding up a finger. Switching to English, he asked, "Did you say we will make movies?"

Michael tossed me another agitated look. That body language shouted out, 'your boss is so dense.' "Yes, yes, that's right. No Oscars, though. We won't be making that kind of film." He grinned toothily and flashed me a wink.

Mr. Sheng did not appear unpuzzled quite yet. "Where would we make these 'films,' as you call them?" he asked.

Michael swept his hands over the table. "Here. I mean, anywhere in the office you want. Whatcha got, maybe 18,000 square feet? Plenty of offices and meeting rooms, and you're using about three that I can tell. Easy to move in the right furniture. A couch, some reclining chairs, an ottoman, a bedroom set."

I'm not the quickest study, but I had a hunch of what Michael might be proposing. Hmm. It was surprising, but he did say that he had pre-screened the concept with Mr. Sheng by phone. I had no idea how this would play with Mr. Sheng, but he was clearly all ears.

After all, Mr. Sheng had been quite direct about what he wanted at our last meeting with Michael: deals with short-term pay-out cycles that can generate cash-flow right away. Michael seemed to be responding to that directive.

"We can film one per week, or do two or three in parallel. Robert can edit one per day, no bottlenecks there, and we'll be paid cash immediately when we deliver the film to the customer."

"Who is the customer?" Mr. Sheng asked.

Michael waved his arm dismissively. "There's more than one. They are close by, just past Hollywood. They pay cash -- $10,000 for about 15 minutes of finished footage." He gave a quick, nervous look at Honey. "Actor salaries average about ten or fifteen percent each, two actors per movie. Robert will take five percent, maybe another five for overhead. The rest is revenue to Coubell, under terms of our commission agreement, of course. You'll easily clear $5,000 per film. I think two a week is achievable, so that's half a million dollars per year."

Mr. Sheng's body language read *I'm very interested*. He was leaning forward in his chair. He also looked very, shall we say, **non**-unpuzzled. "Will we need to host movie stars? Are these comedies? I would like to meet Steve Martin."

The look on Michael's face was priceless. "No! I mean, yes, but you're not going to meet Steve Martin. Tim, can you help here? I explained this on the phone. My Chinese sucks, man."

"OK," I said, "no problem." As the lead

American employee, I was expected to know about the North American market and be able to explain it to my boss. While a stranger to the ways of Hollywood, I felt comfortable improvising, based on what I thought I understood so far.

"So," I informed Mr. Sheng, "in our country, there is a kind of short movie. Steve Martin does longer movies, and he doesn't star in these kinds of films Michael is talking about."

"Who does?" asked Mr. Sheng. "I like Al Pacino." He gave an expectant smile.

This was harder than I had expected. "In these films, we wouldn't expect to see so many famous stars. Except, of course, for people like Honey," I added, hoping not to insult her, but thinking maybe I had.

She smiled. She didn't speak a word, but she was very good at reading the room, too.

"Ah, shit," said Michael. He was glaring at me, but not in any kind of accusatory way. "We talked about this on the phone. I thought he understood. Ah, shit."

I held up a finger. My job. "So, this is the kind of movie that some people – at least, some American people, probably some French people too – like to watch when they are alone. I mean, alone with their wife or husband, or with a date."

"Oh, I know," said Mr. Sheng. "It's a romantic movie." He smiled, I think, because he was proud that he got it. He didn't, though.

Michael bolted out of his chair. "Goddammit," he swore.

I plowed ahead. "Well, yes, very romantic. This type of cinema is really *all* romance. You know, all physical romance."

"Physical?" asked Mr. Sheng.

"Son of a bitch!" swore Michael, then wrapped his arms around his gray blazer, like he was hugging himself, and began loudly smooching the air in front of him, his cheeks and lips reminding me of an actor portraying a fish gulping water to flood its gills.

"Physical romance," he gestured at me, "Just like Tim said. *Very* physical. Goddammit." He shook his head, then plopped back down in his chair.

Mr. Sheng turned to me, his brow now furrowed. "Americans watch this kind of kissing movie?"

"Not just Americans," I clarified. "Europeans, too. Japanese as well. It's possible some Chinese might, I really can't say. We're not talking about just kissing, either." I faced Michael. "Isn't that right, Michael?"

"Shit, Tim," said Michael. "No, of course not, we're not just talking about lip-smacking. We're talking *blue* movies, we're talking the whole show here, full frontal, open kimono. Goddammit, Tim, just tell him already!"

"Right," I said. "You did hear Michael mention bedroom sets, right?"

Mr. Sheng's face slowly rearranged itself. I watched it transmogrify from amused puzzlement into open-mouthed astonishment. Clearly, the light was dawning. He looked over at Honey, who was fiddling with her gold earring and smiling at Mr. Sheng.

"Wahh!" he said, smiling broadly "Wahh! So, she will dance in these movies!" Mr. Sheng faced Honey. "Do you know how to do the Turkish stomach dancing?" he asked, forgetting she didn't know English.

Michael emitted a sudden, loud, "Argh!"

To the extent a thin, gangly man can, Michael now melted. Every limb went flaccid. His arms dropped with a thud on the table, his face fell onto his arms, and then his body slipped out of its chair, and he disappeared completely.

I figured he was ok, but walked around the table to inspect, just in case. He was splayed out on his back on the carpet, eyes closed, mouth open, with a look of constricted pain on his face.

"You ok, buddy?" I asked.

Then he flopped to his left, and sprang up to stand faster than a jack-in-the-box. "No! No, no, no, no, no!!" he implored. "She is not a belly dancer." Michael turned to Honey quickly. "*Are* you a belly dancer?" She just smiled.

"No," he continued, "she's not a belly dancer." He brushed off his suit shoulders. "You're in charge of this now," he said, facing me. "You need to tell him."

This was kind of fun, I thought. And this should be the last time Michael tries to sneak a deal in without first giving me a heads up.

"So," I said. "Super clear now, Mr. Sheng, these movies are not for children. Adults only."

"Adults," said Mr. Sheng. "Adult movies. Oh….Wah…." His ears slowly reddened. His mouth fell open and he fidgeted with his fingers on the table top. "Wah…."

"You got it now?" I asked.

Michael came around the table. He put a reassuring hand on Mr. Sheng's shoulder, and gazed back at me. He screwed up his face into something that my keen sense of body language read as halfway between pride and relief. He gave me a single vigorous nod. I read that as approval for a job well done.

Mr. Sheng looked up directly at me. "We will be in trouble to make these kinds of movies?"

I had no idea.

I'd made few movies – these being amateur Super8 and VHS attempts for friends' weddings and occasional prank films. I'm no Scorsese. And no Scorsese's were needed here.

This was southern California. This was Los Angeles, or close enough. This was Hollywood. The porn capital of the world was in nearby San Fernando Valley. Mr. Sheng didn't know L.A. He knew China, and he knew Harbin, the coldest, most remote, overpopulated and frozen city in China. He knew Beijing. He knew damn well that making this kind of movie would be a questionable endeavor in Beijing.

"I'm talking cash right now," said Michael, swinging back into Mr. Sheng's view. "You said quick cash." His look challenged Mr. Sheng to cross the line.

Mr. Sheng looked at me, nodded his understanding. "Ah, Michael, it is …." His eyes drifted to Honey. She smiled again, and he looked down at the table. "Interesting."

"Don't get hung up on her," Michael said, voice rising loudly, gesturing in Honey's direction. "There will be lots of movies. I mean, she's very pretty, ok." He turned to Honey. "You're very beautiful, very sexy." He faced Mr. Sheng. "I just need you to know that there will be lots of movies, lots of projects.

Many beautiful women. All kinds of women. Even blonde women."

"Wahhh…." said Mr. Sheng. "Wahhh."

Back home in Harbin, Mr. Sheng had a wife and a ten-year-old son. He'd told me how it was for him, being away from his home and family for three months so far, with no idea when he'd get to see them again. He was effectively an unwilling bachelor here. My measure of Mr. Sheng was that he had no intention of *behaving* like a bachelor. Sure, he was struck speechless some mornings when Tamara – the 24-year-old blue-eyed blonde woman he'd hired before me as his office manager entered the office wearing a body-hugging dress or fuzzy sweater. He was not *totally* speechless, actually. He would generally always utter, "Wahhh."

"This deal you have brought us," Mr. Sheng now said. "Very interesting. Please allow me to talk with our headquarters. I think they will have maybe some, it's possible they may, I think, want to ask, they may have—"

"Questions?" asked Michael. "Oh, yeah, they'll have questions, alright." He sighed loudly and looked exhausted.

"Yes," said Mr. Sheng. "I must answer their questions. Michael, do you think it's possible that you and I can talk to our headquarters, together?"

Michael's body froze. He looked as if he'd had his skull cracked with a police baton.

"That won't be necessary," I said. "Mr. Sheng, I think you and I both have a good idea of Michael's project. I'm happy to help answer their questions." I felt like a good Samaritan, getting Michael off the hook. Plus, this was going to be interesting.

"Hmm," said Mr. Sheng. "Very good. Tim and I will discuss with headquarters. We'll get back to you soon, Michael. Thank you for this interesting project. It sounds very profitable."

Michael snapped out of his freeze. "*Zǒu*" he said in Chinese. Let's go. Honey stood. "That's great, Mr. Sheng. Just let me know." He gave me a look that I interpreted as "I shout my astonished disappointment."

I had to shrug at that. Michael had, after all, thrown a curve ball without first signaling. Maybe if he'd warned me of the discussion I could have helped more, but I was also glad he hadn't. I think I'd done the best I could.

We shook hands and waved goodbye to Michael and Honey at the elevator. She was beaming. I think she found the whole thing immensely entertaining. I know I did.

"Tim," Mr. Sheng said. "You are my most important advisor in these matters. How should we proceed? Maybe we call headquarters right now. What do you think?"

OK, I thought. Here we go.

"No, no, I'm just kidding," said Mr. Sheng, laughing. "Wahh, that was amazing. I will call Michael tonight."

"You're sure you don't want to check-in with headquarters?" I said. "You never know, they just might give us the green light." The green light to go into the blue movie biz.

"No," he laughed. "I need to keep my job. If I try to discuss this project with my boss, he will laugh at me like it's a great joke. Until he knows I'm serious."

"Then what?" I asked.

"Why, then he would...." Mr. Sheng regained his face of non-unpuzzlement. "I think he would fire me, but now, maybe I'm thinking more. I'm thinking he might *not* fire me. I think, it is possible, much worse than that."

"Worse than being fired?" I asked. "Is he going to fly over here and break your knee?"

"Oh, no," said Mr. Sheng. "He's a very nice man. No, I'm afraid, you know. Well, you know Mr. Wei. He's a very experienced businessman."

"Sure is," I said. I'd had dinner at his Beijing flat just weeks ago, one of the most beautifully appointed and expensive apartments in the city.

"Hm, yes," continued Mr. Sheng. "You know he's good friends with his neighbor, the famous Jiang YiMou." The Martin Scorsese of China.

"Yes," I said, "he mentioned that. He even stepped across the hall and knocked on Mr. Jiang's door. He wanted to introduce us. Personally, I was hoping Gong Li would answer, but nobody home." At that time, Jiang had been having a live-in affair with the alluring Singapore actress, star of several of Jiang's movies.

"Wah," said Mr. Sheng. "Gong Li."

"Sounds like you're thinking Mr. Wei might just be interested in this idea. Of course, we need to do some research to make sure it's all above board here."

"Wah," said Mr. Sheng, not even close to wearing out that word yet, given the circumstance. "I'm afraid Mr. Wei might say yes. Then we will have to make these adult movies."

"Is that so bad?" I asked. "Sounds very profitable."

"But I am engineer," said Mr. Sheng. "And a businessman."

"There's no business like show business," I informed him. "It's from an old movie, and I think it's true. What's *really* bothering you?"

"You know," he said. "How to explain this to my wife."

I laughed, and gave him a second reassuring pat on the shoulder.

Then it hit me. Oh, crap. How would I explain this to *my* wife?

There was an uncomfortable silence. "Maybe," said Mr. Sheng, "we can suggest to Michael that we can make children's movies, instead."

That settled the matter for me. "We're engineers and businessmen, right? Movies are not our strength. How about we leave that to the pros?"

"Wah…" said Mr. Sheng. I read that as a reluctant yes.

LAS VEGAS

Sugar, Sugar

We met Radisav in the lobby of the Stardust Casino. We'd been connected through Michael, a Chinese American broker we'd worked with on other business. Like all deals he'd brought us, Michael had warned us we'd be dealing with a shadowy group and quirky characters.

"He's Serbian," Michael had said. "And I don't know if this is his culture or just him, but he's really prickly. Try not to piss him off."

This job was like crabbing. I'd haul up my crab cage and get excited about the mass of squirming crustaceans in there, but before I could get it safely on the deck, most of the big ones would slip away.

Deals, deals, everywhere. We were working on ascorbic acid, peanut butter and peanut oil, peanut paste, retail banking software, elevators for the new Beijing Rail station, and fully-depreciated asphalt plants. Apple paste and apple juice from Shandong, polyester scrap recycling, electronic point-of-sale systems, importation of bicycle pumps, exportation of database software, joint ventures for real estate development in China and in New York City; you name it. True, we'd passed on Michael's porn movie production opportunity, and that was probably a good thing. Now, we really needed to get some of chunky deals to round third base. We had orders from the top.

One opportunity kept knocking loudly. For some reason, China was acquiring a sweet tooth. It was probably our fault, here in the States; the Chinese had fallen for KFC and McDonalds, whose red-white buckets and golden arches were erupting in the coastal cities of China. The Chinese seemed to genuinely love KFC – perhaps lured by deference to the Confucian-like gray-haired Colonel. Deep-fried chicken is not exclusively American. The excitement over flash-frozen processed beef? No clue, except kids seemed to love the smiling burger clown.

But sugar? Having lived in Taiwan, I found this very un-Chinese. The only thing that would surprise me more would be a sudden rush on Wisconsin cheddar. During my one year in Taiwan, I'd pined away for cheese. And decent chocolate. OK, and tacos.

"The government of China is buying ship-loads of sugar," said Radisav. Like us, he was here in Las Vegas for a major foreign trade exhibition. "It's a new luxury demand they cannot meet; little domestic supply. Someday, they will grow it in Yunnan or Hainan provinces, maybe. Now, they pay cash."

"We know," said Mr. Sheng. "China needs sugar. Our company would like to buy it."

"Yes," said Radisav, "every Chinese wheeler dealer says that. Demand is high, the risks great. Can you perform?"

"We can," said Mr. Sheng, and I sensed he was

now in his element, leaning forward toward Radisav in his chair. "You tell us, Ratsave, what you need."

"Radisav!" shouted the Serbian, hitting fist to table top.

"Ratisave."

"Rad-i-sav!" shouted Radisav.

"Yes, Mr. Radison," said Mr. Sheng. "Our company will provide whatever you need."

Radisav's face was red, and he turned to glare at me. I shrugged my shoulders, and Radisav sighed loudly.

"We need a general, irrevocable, letter of credit," he said. "Issued by Hong Kong or British bank. No Bank of China! And it must be payable under our exact terms. Once it is opened, I can arrange shipment. The ship holds 12,500 metric tons. INCOTERMS are Ex-Works, of course."

Mr. Sheng knew INCOTERMS. So did I. We'd both just learned them in the past few weeks. Seemed everything we did required such knowledge. INCOTERMS are internationally recognized terms of delivery: who pays for shipping, who owns and insures the goods during transport, and such not. Ex-Works was, of course, the harshest possible on the buying party, and seldom used.

"Can we split the Ex-Works?" Mr. Sheng asked.

"What?" asked Radisav, grimacing in puzzlement. "Whuttt?"

"He means," I clarified, "can we split shipping costs. You know, can we go Dutch?"

"Yes," said Mr. Sheng. "We ask for Dutch."

Radisav rubbed his head as if to massage away a sudden headache. "Fuck off."

"OK," said Mr. Sheng. "That's nice of you."

I think he must have heard "half-off." Hand-signaling Radisav for a pause, I whispered in Mr. Sheng's ear. "No, no, he said he *won't* split the shipping fees. I think the bigger problem is insurance, since we technically own the sugar even before it starts the journey. What if the ship sinks?" Mr. Sheng's shoulders perked up at this.

"Is your ship safe?"

"It's not my ship," said Radisav, "but I would say no, it's not safe. That's why you need very good insurance. You will own the goods long before they even get onto the ship. You should ask if the crane that lifts the sugar is safe. No, it's not safe, either. Is the truck driver who brings the sugar to the shipyard reliable? No, they are all bandits, they will rob your goods if they can, damage or taint them if they want. All this is *your* problem, not mine. I get paid before anything happens.

"You guys are new to this, I see. I only work with competent partners. I think you're not that."

"Our company is very reliable," said Mr. Sheng. "Let us show you." My cue: I flipped open my laptop.

"No," said Radisav, "no stupid slideshows. You know how difficult it is to get a shipload of sugar right now. Do you want to do business or don't you?"

"How much?" I asked.

"Spot price," said Radisav. "Plus all costs. Plus 20% for my efforts. Tell me port of delivery."

"Yantai," said Mr. Sheng, a fierce gleam in his eye. "We take all our commodities at Yantai."

I had to look that one up later. It's a small port in Shandong province, directly across the Yellow Sea from Korea.

"Right now," said Radisav, "market price for sugar is $280 per metric ton, plus our fee, plus full inbound, loading, and transport costs." He tapped out a few numbers on his calculator. "We need irrevocable LC for $4.8 million. Spot fluctuates daily, so call it $5.5 million."

"Wahhh…" said Mr. Sheng.

Radisav looked puzzled. "What does that mean?"

"Mr. Sheng means, no problem," I said.

Recovering, Mr. Sheng shook his head in the affirmative. "Wahhh…."

We phoned our banker that afternoon from Mr. Sheng's hotel room. "Sacre bleu," he said, with his thick Parisian accent. "Yes, certainly we can issue this kind of LC, but are you sure?"

"It's a problem?" asked Mr. Sheng.

"Well, it's very risky," said the banker. "This type of financial instrument is rarely used. Irrevocable means just that. We don't do these very often. You could be left holding the bag, you know. Once we issue this instrument, the money is gone, poof! No recourse. Gone with the wind."

"We will buy insurance," said Mr. Huang.

"Do you have an agent?" the banker asked. "I can line you up with Jeremiah at Lloyds. My guess is this will be an expensive policy. Maybe 15% or 20%."

"Wahhh…"

"If he'll even write it," continued the banker. "This one is pretty chilling. Can't you negotiate him to a DDP price?" which is Delivered Duty Paid.

"He'll charge more, but then he's responsible for delivery all the way to Yantai."

Mr. Sheng looked at me. He knew I was as out of my element as he was. We weren't finance guys. We were engineers. I wasn't a very good engineer, which is why I was now a businessman. My guess is that Mr. Sheng was a far better engineer. And yet, right now, he was an amateur businessman like me.

We finished the chat with our banker. Mr. Sheng informed me. "You must negotiate with Ratsave."

"Radisav," I said.

"Tell him 'no' to this irrevocable LC. We must have DDP, and protections to both sides."

"Seems reasonable," I said. "Are you sure you want *me* to tell him?"

"Yes. I can't understand his English. What kind of English is that anyway?"

"Serbian English," I said.

"Well," said Mr. Sheng, "it's wrong. He should speak English better. Like me. Talk to him. I will call headquarters in Beijing, get more ideas."

I had my marching orders. I stepped out and placed a call to Radisav's mobile phone.

"Hey, it's Tim from Coubell."

"What is a fucking Cowbell?" asked Radisav; a reasonable question. It was something about cooperation universally making a happy bell-like noise. I dodged the question and reminded him of our meeting earlier that morning.

"Ah," he said. "The Chinese guys. Except you. American guy who thinks he's Chinese. What do you need?"

"I'm wondering if we can talk about a different kind of LC for the sugar deal?"

"Oh," said Radisav, "so you don't trust me. Then see if you can find someone else to sell you sugar."

"Nothing like that at all," I said, only lying because it was the business-like thing to do. "We have confidence you can deliver. Our banker suggested—"

"I don't do business with people who let their bankers kick them around," said Radisav sharply. "Look, you give me the irrevocable LC, I make a call to Cyprus, and a really big ship breaks anchor and starts out immediately. I mean today, tonight, to get your sugar and deliver it to Yantai."

"You mean," I asked, "the sugar is already onboard?"

"What?" asked Radisav. "Fuck no, man. It will go get your sugar in the Caribbean, head straight through the Panama Canal, and you'll have your goods in under a fortnight. Who *else* can do that for you? No fucking *one*, that's the name of the who else."

Caribbean. I vaguely heard a bell, though it was not a happy sound. It was more of an alarm bell.

I asked, "What's the nation of origin—"

"Look," said Radisav. "You and I are just the goddamn brokers, ok? We make the deal. You think your commie Chinese customer cares about my freakin' Cuban supplier? If you do, then you're not real, and then I say 'Fuck you.'"

"Oh, we're real," I assured him. That, too, was a lie in the name of being business-like. I actually had no idea how *real* we were. I knew that I couldn't screw up the deal. Though I really hoped my boss would screw it up instead, because I wanted nothing to do with giving Radisav $5.5 million to violate U.S. trade restrictions; not to mention the possibility that his "ship" might sail away with nothing but our cash to celebrate their successful scam with a few fabulously expensive nights in Monte Carlo.

"Well, ok," he said. "These ship captains are opportunists. I can only tell you first-come, first-served. Get me an LC by morning and you'll be happy. Otherwise, you are nothing to me. *Nothing*!"

"Any chance we can meet for dinn—" Click.

I thought the call had gone fairly well. At least, I think Radisav had made himself clear. I took a deep breath and went back up to Mr. Sheng's room.

"Tim, did you negotiate the LC?" asked Mr. Sheng. "How about a price reduction?"

Sigh. "Well, given Radisav's general inflexibility, I don't believe we can expect a price reduction."

"Hmm. That's too bad. Sugar is expensive. How about the terms? Ratsave seems like a reasonable man."

"Radisav," I corrected again. "Very reasonable. Very direct. Most important in business, right?"

"Most important," agreed Mr. Sheng. "So he will Dutch us on the shipping charges?"

My poker hand in this discussion with my boss was a loser. It was time to slap down all the cards, face-up. "Well, I'm not sure we can do this deal with Radisav."

Mr. Sheng shook his head. "We need this deal. Ratsave charges high commission, but our office will pay us for the trouble. Eight percent of net purchase value. That's $360,000. Remember, your commission is 7% of office profits, so your share …"

"Is half my annual salary," I informed him. "I

hope yours is bigger."

"Of course," he said. "I'm the boss."

"The problem is," I said, "even if we trust Radisav, his supply chain sounds unreliable. Sounds like the shippers are licensed pirates. And no, he won't change terms at all."

Mr. Sheng was quiet. "I don't trust the deal either. That's why the terms must be mutual, half-risk, half-risk. But you say he won't consider it."

"No, he won't. And there's one more thing you should know. He plans to get the sugar from Cuba."

"Really?" said Mr. Sheng. "Oh, that's interesting. Very high quality." Which didn't sound right, since Mr. Sheng knew well about US restrictions on trade with Cuba.

"As a U.S. branch office," I reminded him, "we can't touch Cuban sugar. We can't even smoke a Cuban cigar."

"Don't worry," said Mr. Sheng. "I don't smoke. And…" he smiled broadly, stood, and rubbed his hands together.

"Yes? And?"

"And," he said, "you will like this news…we have found a *new* supplier! We don't need Ratsave."

"Radisav." Now this was a huge load off my shoulders. "Who is this new supplier?"

"I just spoke with our commodity manager in Beijing." And now Mr. Sheng's face was all aglow.

"Really? If he found the supplier—"

"I know, I know," said Mr. Sheng, "normally, that means no commission to us. It's our job to find the supplier. Good try with your friend from Brazil, and too bad it didn't work. Then, Michael introduced us to Ratsave, but, well, he's not a good guy for us."

"But now," said Mr. Sheng, smiling broadly, "headquarters has found a good supplier, and they agreed to give us our commission, anyway! They want to recognize our efforts, so we can be motivated for all other deals we are working."

That was brilliant! I thought. No work, no risk, no sweating for two weeks while our "ship" might or might not be on course. And the commission! I started thinking about paying down my mortgage early, maybe a new set of wheels for my wife's birthday.

"The sugar will come from Hainan Island," said Mr. Sheng.

Hainan? That was a Chinese province near Taiwan. "How does that work?" I asked.

"Well," he explained, "I told them about the 12,500 metric tons. Seems they don't need that much. And quality is not a problem, so no need for Cuban or Hawaiian."

"OK, how much do they need?"

"Eight tons," beamed Mr. Sheng.

"Eight…tons? You sure it's not *8,000* tons?"

"No, just eight," he said. "And the best part, it's cheaper! Only $130 per ton."

So, there. We'd made a deal. We had a *crab in the cage on deck*. We'd just bought $1,040 dollars of cheap sugar sent from one Chinese port to another, and our office had earned $83 for our troubles. My share would be $5.82. Good-bye new car. Oh, well, I thought. Far better than being at risk to the Serbian Mafia and US Department of Commerce.

"Let's grab some dinner," said Mr. Sheng. "Any food you want. As long as it's Dutch."

"You want Dutch food for dinner?" I cocked my

head, wearing my non-unpuzzled face.

"Pay with Dutch style," he added.

Mr. Sheng was a quick study and a shrewd businessman. There went my commission.

LAS VEGAS

Suits Us Fine

"Look at those," Mr. Sheng said, waving me forward. This trade exhibition had already yielded us a number of interesting matches for deals we were working. We'd found a joint venture partner for industrial tools, a potential channel for electrical harnesses and wiring bundles our electronics subsidiary assembled, and a buyer for plastics and chemicals from our factory in Hubei province. I fast followed Mr. Sheng through the crowded floor so as not to lose him again.

That would be annoying. The show was thriving and crowded, and I had no idea what was so interesting here. He disappeared into a booth and was nearly swallowed up by racks of men's suits and jackets.

I caught up as he was fingering a blue blazer. "Wah, good material. Nice stitching."

"What do we need with cheap suits?" I asked.

"No, these are high quality. This is just what we need." It was true the company was doing a million different things at once, but men's clothing….?

"There is strong demand in China for American made clothing," he explained. "Not cheap clothes, but high-end suits and women's wear."

"Interesting," I observed. It made sense – with so many American products catching fire in China. Everything from GMC vehicles to Kentucky Fried Chicken – why not American clothing brands. Levi's jeans were a huge hit. Yet, something wasn't adding up.

"I didn't know there were any American suit makers left," I noted. Mr. Sheng ignored me, as he searched a pair of trousers to find the manufacturer's label.

"Can I help you?" said a young man, dressed in one of his own products. He had starched white cuffs with gold cufflinks protruding at the GQ prescribed length past his coat sleeves. His black dress shoes were brilliantly shined. He wore a professional business smile below his black 1980s Miami Vice styled haircut.

"Where are these suits made?" Mr. Sheng asked.

"Are you Chinese?" the man asked, and smiled more broadly. "These are expertly cut and sewn in Yunnan Province," he said in Chinese. At least I think that's what I heard, because Mr. Sheng grunted in disgust.

"Wah, China?" said Mr. Sheng. "Don't you have any American suits?"

The man studied Mr. Sheng's face, then mine. "We can arrange that," he said.

"You can?" asked Mr. Sheng.

"Oh, yes, that's no problem at all."

"Ah, that's nice!" said Mr. Sheng. "That's what we need."

My personal alarm bell was ringing. Wait, really? I thought. You buy from an American manufacturer? Or you just put "Made In America" labels on these?

The man smiled, tilted his head. "How many do you need?" he asked. "We can have 500 ready by tomorrow night."

I turned to Mr. Sheng, whose eyes were wide. "How much?" he asked the salesman.

"Twenty-five dollars per suit, complete with slacks and coat. I can get you a three piece, toss in the vest, for another $8. These can sell in China for $60 to $80. American quality."

Mr. Sheng's mouth was open. "Wahhh."

I felt the need to throw some cold water on both of these fellows. "Guys," I said, "You're both from China, right?"

"Yes," they answered.

"And you both want to do international business, right?"

"Right," said Mr. Sheng.

"Of course," said the salesman.

"Then you can't just trade with *each other*."

Mr. Sheng appeared mystified, but our suit salesman laughed knowingly.

It took a few minutes, but Mr. Sheng finally, reluctantly, agreed. We exchanged cards and bid adieu with our "Made In America" suit salesman.

"It's a shame," said Mr. Sheng, as we continued our amble through the sprawling trade show. "We could have made a nice business."

"New English phrase for you, Mr. Sheng. 'This business is not suitable for our company.'"

"Suitable? Oh, very good. I see. Ha! OK, let's go find some suitable business."

"Suits me fine," I responded.

"Suits everyone fine," he laughed. "I like English more every day."

Indeed, it suited us all very well, in every sense. Particularly in the sense that it allowed us to avoid a *law suit*.

FUN AND GAMES

PHUKET, THAILAND

The International Incident

"Well," said Chris. "We're completely cluster-fucked now."

"Such language!" I said, gunning our rental jeep toward the next tourist goal-post, the lively market and temple at Wat Chalong. "What's the problem? Everything's golden, you're nearly recovered, and our buddy will land in time to join us for dinner. Another dinner in paradise, I might add."

It had been a relaxing morning of casual sightseeing in the jeep, reconnoitering Phuket Island's tropical treelined hills and ivory sand beaches. We took it easy as Chris was still recovering from the worst sunburn of his life. It had happened four days ago in the blink of an eye, while we reclined on these beaches, such was the ferocity of nearly equatorial ultra-violet.

"Dinner is off," said Chris. "Cary is going to slaughter us both." I glanced from the road to see he was reviewing a sheet of paper, then I returned my vigilance where it belonged, the ever unpredictable frenzied island traffic. The paper contained Cary's itinerary, which we'd both consulted and double-checked this morning. His flight was due from Tokyo at 6:00 pm, and it was only noon. The airport was just a few minutes away from almost every point on the island.

"Issue?" I asked.

"Says here he landed at zero six hundred."

"No, no," I corrected. "We both confirmed. It says six pm. No?"

"No," said Chris. "Says here he left Tokyo at 23:00. That's military time."

"So?"

"Turn it around there," Chris pointed to a widening in the road. There were fast-moving tuk-tuks coming in both directions, but I did as instructed, applied a little brake, then swung the wheel hard, emitting a squeal of tires that any movie maker shooting a chase scene would have to admire. We were now headed back the way we'd come.

But I'd cut it very tight with a fast flying tuk-tuk now closing from behind, and cringed as the squeal of its brakes and loud blast on the horn signaled the driver's displeasure. The horn persisted and blared with a force far out of proportion to the tiny three-wheeled motorized cycle being piloted. The sound was so ominous, I slowed.

The tuk-tuk whizzed by, the driver still leaning into his horn, creating a solid doppler effect – *vvvvvrrrrraaaaannnnnggggg* – as he zoomed past us. To my surprise, he was smiling and gave a pleasant wave, despite the fact that I'd threatened his life with that crazy stunt.

"The Thais are so nice," I exalted. "Back in L.A. we'd be evading pistol fire over that kind of move."

"Well get ready to be shot on sight," reminded Chris. "We're in a heap of trouble."

"How could we have screwed the pooch?" I implored, speeding up and carefully passing the same tuk-tuk with plenty of clearance. The driver and I both waved giddily at each other. I've never been so deeply in love with a country.

"Military time," said Chris. "Since it says here the flight left Tokyo at 23:00, *all* these times must also be military. Zero six hundred means he landed hours ago."

"Hell no!" I said. "It does *not* say 'zero' six hundred! We both looked it over."

"True," said Chris. "It's a FUBAR by the travel agency. They left off the leading zero. Doesn't matter. It adds up, Tokyo to Phuket can't be much more than seven, eight hours tops. Tokyo is ahead two hours, his flight left at 8:00pm Phuket time, it's now nearly noon. Crap, he's been on the ground here for more than five or six hours. We are so clustered."

"OK, our bad. He'll forgive us," I assured.

Chris gave me a dirty sidelong glance.

"Well, he'll forgive us *someday*," I corrected. "That's what I meant."

I knew what Chris was thinking. I was thinking it too.

It had only been six months now since "The Incident." The Incident would seem to be a highly predictive indicator of how much trouble we were now about to pick up at the Phuket airport, assuming the poor guy had dutifully waited lo these six hours for us to come get him. Not that he had much choice. We had no pre-arranged hotels, and were in fact staying in a thatched hut on Karon Beach that had no address, near as I knew. The mobile phone was still something glamorous found only in big brick style or welded to the dashboards of the Hollywood legal set.

"The Incident." We hadn't expected it, not from a guy like Cary. Now, given the immediate sorry state of affairs, we couldn't realistically expect anything other than a repeat. One that, as the painful memory manifested for me, I thought might come to be known as "The *International* Incident."

Cary was a lawyer. One day he intended to become a judge. A strict proceduralist, he was an ardent adherent to Common Law that issued from the Magna Carta, and he believed the Napoleonic Codification of legality is the true lasting legacy of French Colonialism. When Cary cited legal precedence, he could also trace it back to the specific dates and venues at which the case law had been born.

And not just the big cases, like Brown vs. Board of Education and Plessy vs. Ferguson, and Socrates vs. the Athenian State; he could cite obscurities like Sears-Roebuck vs. Smith (in which Mr. Smith won on Illinois Superior Court appeal regarding a lawnmower he'd been sold with dull blades). I knew this stuff, because Cary told us all about it, whether we were interested or not.

He was a speed-reader, an omnivorous all-devouring consumer of the written word. With his eidetic memory and immense power of reasoning, there was no topic upon which he could not effectively discourse, with the potential exception of European Field Hockey. Notwithstanding the foregoing, he navigated with confidence and aplomb across literature, science, history, cinema, politics and philosophy, while operating openly and solely upon the honor system.

By almost any measure, Cary was a renaissance man without flaw. Some measures must be exempted, however, and not just the Field Hockey business. Softball and hoops were absent from his toolkit, and he was positively dangerous with a Frisbee. While lacking in athletic prowess, his considerable list of merits were crowned with the curious phenomenon of his naivety; it was endearing, if an awkward confluence in one gifted with limitless intelligence.

The result was that Cary was convinced that I, too, was as mentally agile as he. As if this weren't sufficiently misguided, he also believed that *everyone* was his intellectual equal. Like the Director of Intelligence from the film "Zero Dark Thirty" he was emphatic that "We're all smart!" Which I also believe is true. Just not all at the same level and in the exact same ways. All the time. And definitely not like Cary.

And while this view of his was charming and egalitarian, it led to misunderstandings. "The Incident" being the most awkward to date.

It had happened just a few months previous to our mis-timed rendezvous at Phuket airport. Two contingents of friends, one nominally led by Cary and the other by Chris, had agreed to meet in San Francisco on a Sunday morning. We'd convene at the parking structure in Chinatown and walk together to our favorite dim sum venue. The plan: be at the restaurant early, since tables were plentiful from opening at 10:00am but would be choked with clientele by 11:00am – with astounding consistency. Any later, and one had, best case, a 50/50 shot at being served before the onset of hypoglycemic shock and cardiac arrest.

Our plan would put us all in the restaurant 45 minutes before the rush. A great plan, with built-in buffer time. Our parents had not spent all that money on college for nothing, now had they?

If "The Incident" – and moreover, "The International Incident" – had occurred just a year later, they would have been negated by Cary's acquisition of a pager. With no mobile device, it was incumbent upon the leaders of the two groups to adhere to the plan. Even when the plan went wrong.

Both groups, nine in all, had arrived on time at the parking structure. One had gone downstairs, the other up. That's San Francisco. Festooned with steep hills, there were exits at ground level in both directions, at different altitudes. Chris and I waited up-top with our group in the park where Chinese seniors practiced their tai chi. We were unaware that Cary and his team were waiting just a hundred meters away, down below, at the entrance to the parking structure – waiting and watching the incoming vehicles for us to show.

At 10:30, Chris made the command decision. "Given the crowd risk, it's logical to presume they went ahead to the restaurant. Either they're late and will catch-up, or they're already there waiting for us. Let's go."

My growling stomach reinforced this logic. It was unassailable. Duty and low blood sugar now joined forces in the virtuous quest of staking out a spot where we might drive our chopsticks into steaming shrimp dumplings to be dipped into spicy sauces, and to tear tender steamed *cha-shu bao* filled with slightly sweetened pork, to be chased with strong, hot Oolong tea. Besides, orders are orders, ours was not to reason why.

In just a few minutes, we were at the restaurant. No sign of our gang. It was filling quickly. Chris tried to stakeout a table large enough for all nine of us.

"You nine people?" asked the host. "Where? I see five. Table for five." And we were seated, anticipating the others would show momentarily and claim an adjacent table. Meantime, the little food carts were flying thick and fast, driven with urgency by Chinese women of a certain seniority, as is the case in dim sum establishments, it seems, the world over. We began the feast.

In minutes, every table was full. Halfway through our repast, still no sign of our friends, there was a full waiting room, and shortly thereafter, a line of waiting diners down the sidewalk. We had no clue what had become of Cary as we reached satiation and began turning away the little carts of food.

And that's when Cary, red-faced and sweating, stormed up to our table, trailed by his entourage. The restaurant was loud with clanking dishes, rolling carts and animated conversation until it was loud with just one sound.

"*You!*" Cary shouted louder than one would have imagined possible, his deep bass vibrato bouncing off the walls of the restaurant, pointing squarely at Chris. "All of you!" The finger moved to each us in turn. "You're all goddamned *mother*—"

Perhaps I'll just summarize the text of his speech. You could have heard a pin drop when he paused to inhale. He commanded the floor, so to say. Spittle flew and arms waved. Twice, he paused to adjust his dark-rimmed glasses, which kept threatening to leap off his face.

It was glorious, it was ghastly, and it was passionate. In summation, Cary rendered his verdict. We were all, more or less, while still his cherished friends, officially in his dog house. "You broke trust! I may forgive, but I'll *never* forget!"

To his credit, Chris waited until the fulmination was essentially over before mentioning that there had been a flaw in our jointly conceived rendezvous plan, and we had done what we'd deemed the logical thing.

"Cary," Chris had said, "given the breakdown in our plan, it was my duty to salvage the prospects of the team under my direct command. The needs of the many outweigh the needs of the few, and the fewer." Chris had led five, Cary four. I held my breath, expecting this to re-ignite the flames of Cary's anger.

Instead, Cary paused. He readjusted his glasses. Then he nodded his head in agreement while glancing around the table at our well-fed faces, and then around the restaurant at all the very full tables, where folks had begun to resume their brunch and speak amongst themselves again.

"Logical," said Cary. "You raise a good point." His unstoppable reason had bested his anger. For a brief moment. Then his face flushed cherry red again.

"*Traitors!* " He bellowed, wheeled and stormed outside. His cohort gave an embarrassed shrug, and dutifully followed him out.

Time had healed the mutual wounding. But it was several weeks before any of us could laugh about it, and nobody had had the nerve to re-visit this event directly with Cary.

"Well and truly clustered," said Chris, as I down-shifted the jeep into the Phuket airport parking lot. I engaged the hand brake and we jumped out. We double-timed in silence toward the terminal building and our anticipated rendezvous with justice.

Really, what would *I* have done if left stranded in a foreign airport for six hours with no idea when or if rescue would arrive?

The answer quickly became apparent, and it made some sense. I could see familiar brown hair and thick dark-rim glasses bent over the final pages of a large hardcover book. Cary sat on the ground, back against the terminal building, a small satchel next to him. "Cary!" I shouted, much as Mark Hammill did, though by mistake, at the triumphant scene in Star Wars Episode IV (he meant to say, "Leia!").

Cary looked up, spotted us approaching. He dog-eared the page, and exploded onto his feet. I was prepared for the verbal flogging of my life, but I took one shot at pre-emption. I threw myself at the mercy of the court, you might say.

"We screwed up huge, we thought you were coming in—"

"About time you got here, Jenkins." He reached out and shook my hand, a big smile on his face. "Admiral," he said to Chris, since that's what we all called Chris back then. The Admiral. Of the Fleet. Long story. Could be a Star Trek thing.

"So," said Chris. "You're not going to skin us alive?" I detected some hint of disappointment in his voice.

"Hey," said Cary, "shit happens. I'll forgive you both if you buy me a Singha – *each* – at dinner tonight. By the way, Jenkins, I'm about done with this." He handed me his copy of Tom Clancy's *The Sum of All Fears*. "You'll like it," he said. "I was re-reading the last two chapters again, so you got here just in time."

The sum of all fears. I admit, I'd been scared half out of my socks at what Cary would do when we finally rescued him. I'd been ready for anything, except for what he did, which was to slap us playfully on the shoulder here and there on the drive back to our beach bungalow in paradise, causing Chris to wince in a most un-Shatner-like non-Shakespearean manner, due to his still healing sunburn. Cary was genuinely ecstatic to see us.

After we'd made good a few times on our pledge of Singha at dinner, I worked up the nerve to ask.

"So Cary, why in hell did you publicly thrash us at the dim sum place last summer, and today – after stranding you alone in a foreign country for hours – did you *not* thrash us again?"

Cary held up his index finger, requesting patience as he munched a giant chunk of dripping barbequed swordfish meat, and masticated with evident enjoyment the requisite fourteen cycles. He came up for air and let rip a hearty burp.

"Totally different paradigm, Jenkins," he said "No relation whatsoever."

"Really?" asked Chris. "How so?"

The lawyer Cary went into high gear. "In both situations, an innocent error was made. Culpability is not demonstrable. However, in the former incident," his tirade that offended half of Chinatown in a purely collateral side effect, "as the leader of the team, my command was humiliated in front my troops – and fellow commander." He tipped his fork to Chris. "I lost face, and I reacted in a human, if uncivilized, manner."

Mystery solved. Beating averted. Face saved. From that dinner we went on to enjoy many adventures together on the peninsular islands of Thailand, and on and under the Andaman sea. I finished reading the *Sum of All Fears*. Ours had added to naught.

JAPAN

Hive Mentality

Hakata.

What in the world was I doing here? I'd stepped out of the train station at Hakata, on Japan's major southern island of Kyushu. Hakata, also known as Fukuoka, is a small city. According to the guidebook, there wasn't a lot to recommend it, though it had been an alternate target for Little Boy if the weather over Nagasaki had been inclement that fateful day in August 1945.

From my perch at the top of the railway stairs, I scanned the gloomy July skyline, and rain fogged my glasses. It was 3:55pm. Another Tokyo-bound Shinkansen would arrive in seven minutes. Hakata or Tokyo for the night? Even though Tokyo was 1,100km and five hours away on the bullet train, Tokyo still sounded better. I snapped a photo of the general Hakata metro area and ran back inside the station.

I'd be in Roppongi by 9:30pm, courtesy of my Japan Rail pass. Foreign tourists can buy these passes ahead of arrival in Japan. While not cheap, they enable the visitor unfettered access to ride just about any train going anywhere. Travelers go anytime they want, anywhere they want, as much as they want.

I was determined to get full value on my J-RAIL pass. I'd met up with friends in Shizuoka and

Nagoya, seen the heart-rending museum at Hiroshima, the majesty of Himeji Castle and the lily-pad bordered serenity of the Golden Pavilion, Kinjakuji. I was burning up the rails, on full galavant, across the Land of the Rising Sun.

The ride from Hakata to Tokyo was surreal. Traveling at over 200km per hour is akin to threading urban canyons in a pre-WWII fixed-wing monoplane – except quieter. The eye is drawn to distant scenery as everything close by is moving too fast. I enjoyed the sunset near Mt. Fuji, and caught a light snack in the elevated dining car. I even made it through a few chapters of the latest Robert Ludlum novel.

From Tokyo Station, I rode the subway a few stops, and exited into a cool evening on the far-side of dusk. The night was ablaze with behemoth neon signs and giant video screens.

Roppongi is Tokyo's most notable district for great food, music, and nightlife. I set out for an inexpensive pension at which I'd stayed previously. It had been no problem getting a room there on short notice. On the way, something caught my eye, and hunger interdicted.

The "Hofbrau House in Munich in Tokyo," that's how I read the sign of this intriguing establishment. There was German food with German beer minutes from my hotel.

Entering the Hofbrau was like squeezing through a teleporter. I slipped the ordered bonds of Tokyo and emerged into the lively musical chaos of an Octoberfest evening. While the corseted and well-muscled fräuleins carrying multiple steins of beer were all Japanese, it was a dead-ringer for its namesake in Munich. Guests shared wooden tables and benches, and a genuine German "oompah" band was knocking out a polka. You could cut the schnitzel in the air with a sausage clever. After days of sashimi and yakitori, I'd been transported into the land of the *Schlachteplatte* and apple streusel. My stomach emitted a premonitory growl.

A fräulein put a hand on my shoulder. "Dinner?"

Not "dinner for one," I noted. She led me to a well-populated wooden table, where every diner had an enormous stein of sudsy beer. Some, apparently European, sang along with the band. Most were locals. I received hearty welcomes from my tablemates as the fräulein guided me to a spot on the bench with just enough room between my compadres to receive one enormous beer stein and one generous *schlachteplatte*.

Both arrived quickly. In the interim, I'd made fast friends with my tablemates: a young couple from Hamburg, newlyweds from Kanazawa prefecture, and three women celebrating one's engagement.

The German fare did a full reset on my taste buds. While I love Japanese dishes, so much of the same for so long had masked a latent desire for a heartier fare that the sizzling smells of the Hofbrau promised with a vengeance. The *schlachteplatte* – "slaughter plate" in English – included six different German sausages and four intensely flavorful mustards. These were in concentric rings surrounding a purple mass of sauerkraut. It was a Teutonic feast.

The band was on a streak, and they, too, had steins from which they sucked impossibly large draughts after each song. The very next one they played must have been popular as the entire restaurant erupted with the first chord.

Even the waitstaff deferred their frenetic serving to join in. Our waitress grabbed my hand and led me onto the dance floor, into the conga line. The normally reserved polite demeanor of Japanese folks was apparently checked at the door in this venue, and it was a gala, frenetic soiree.

I do not know how to dance. The whole thing scares me, as I suspect at any instant I'm apt to rain down violent accidental orthopedic damage on myself or my fellow dancers. I am that clumsy.

Somehow, I was in the groove. I did what our fräulein did. She'd now taken the lead and placed my left hand on her shoulder. With that, and guidance from the hand of the person behind me, the prospect of choreographic cataclysm was all but forgotten. I was dancing and actually having fun. I never had before, perhaps never will again. After a fast and furious few minutes, the band finished the tune with an accordion flourish and we returned to our tables. The raucous applause began to mellow, and –

OOMPAH! OOMPAH! – music erupted again.

About 11:00pm, I determined it would be prudent to bid adieu and check into my nearby pension. It was a hug-fest getting out the door, but hugs are known dopamine generators, and I was feeling on top of the world as I covered the two blocks to my hotel.

Unfortunately, it *wasn't* my hotel.

"Oh, sorry, sir, tonight we fill-up just now. You know, last train gone."

For the working men and women who lived far outside the city center – which was most – the mandatory company bonding, sales dinners and drink-a-thons generally ended in time for the final train. The boss was respectful that sleep, even if not an actual personal life, was a fringe benefit the company should bestow on its employees.

Yet sometimes, say the boss has just been promoted and wants to celebrate, and a million other reasons that would crop up with alarming frequency for tired "salarymen" and "office ladies" alike, the last train was just a kicking off point for all-night revelry. Everybody did it, because being a team player is a Japanese corporate imperative.

"Hotel full," the clerk added.

"OK," I said, thinking that it *was* ok. I seldom went anywhere without reservations, and this was turning into the adventure I'd been missing. "Are there any other hotels nearby?"

The clerk frowned a true frowny face, a squinch-of-the-nose and suck-in-of-the-cheeks level frown. "No, you misunderstand," he said, "no hotel rooms left in city."

"Alright," I said.

"You can stay in hive," he said, pointing at a map taped to his counter. "Hive will take you."

"Hive?" I asked. "What is the hive?"

"You stay there," he said, and picked up his phone. He delivered some terse Japanese embedded into which was the word "gaijin" so they knew who to expect.

I followed the clerk's instructions through several blocks of now darkening downtown, as pubs and restaurants switched off their neon signs for the night. I passed my goal without noticing, but a uniformed man chased me down the street. "Gaijin? Here!"

Were it not for the clerk's call I would have dawdled into the Tokyo dawn. Instead, I was reeled into the Hive.

At the reception desk, the same man provided a leather folio with an invoice for 3,800 yen, about $40 dollars. A downtown Tokyo hotel room on short notice at that price was a bargain, I thought, not yet realizing that the Hive was no ordinary hotel.

The clerk pointed me down a hallway, that led to a locker room. A large man who had to weigh two hundred fifty pounds and might have been as many years old grunted and pointed me to locker 2112. He tossed me a white robe, then watched as I doffed my clothing and consigned all my possessions into the locker. The sensei made a big show handing me the key, demonstrating the number, how to hold it, how to insert in the correct orientation, and then twist clockwise.

He gestured; I followed. We passed through a hallway and into a room that reminded me of a particular dungeon from the video game 'Doom,' the one stacked floor-to-ceiling with identical rectangular panels. Here, the panels were openings.

"You, up," he said and gestured up, way up, with his eyes. There were metal footholds leading upward and vertical bars to facilitate climbing. I clambered up, passing 2112A, 2112B and 2112C without waking a mouse, then wriggled into the sarcophagus of 2112D, just below the ceiling. I crawled in.

At the back was a pillow. The entire "room" was a bed with neat white sheets, the pillow, and a mounted tv screen apparently sized for viewing by hobbits, angled on the "ceiling" of the room for viewing when one's head was on the pillow. There was an AM-FM radio with 1970s automotive style controls, and a switch for lights. All easily accessible while lying on my back, which was perfect, given there was not enough clearance to sit-up. What more could one need?

I watched an hour of Japanese soap opera while the novelty wore off and I grew sleepy. I could hear snores and a few times a fellow tenant noisily climbed up or down to hit the community latrine.

The Hive! Sure enough, we were bees in a beehive, aka "capsule hotel." The Japanese, and let no one from here to Timbuktu try to tell you otherwise, are really clever. They'd solved the late night drunken office worker commuter crisis by creating sardine can solutions that actually felt like cozy, comfy homes away from home. I took pleasure in the compact genius before I drifted into sleep.

A loud klaxon startled me awake.

Fire? My watch read 5:30am. There were moans, there were groans, there were cries of *"Ohayo! Ohayo gozaimasu!"* – good morning shouted at such ferocity as to be the Gong of Heaven. The same large, wizened sensei was deftly climbing up and down to each and every opening in the honeycomb to ensure its worker bee was extracted.

I like to think I didn't squeal the way some of the other guys did – guys (hives are either all men or all women) who'd barely fallen asleep, many of whom still had DUI-levels of blood alcohol.

We were all the same: fatigued, drunken men rousted awake, stripped of our robes and thrust naked into the not-so-warm group shower – the kind where I had felt the sharp sting of whip-like wet towels snapping at my buttocks in middle school gym class – while listening to an automated warning message in Japanese, which I learned was: "Final shower is 5:45. One towel each, please."

It was a re-processing facility where exhausted "salarymen" were being recycled into shocked-awake salarymen. The one towel was small, and it had to used quickly, as it was evident we'd be ejected imminently.

Breaking a sweat as I pulled on my socks and shoes, I was nearly the last to get the heave-ho. It was 5:57am. I was wet behind the ears and back on the streets of Tokyo, with nowhere to go.

I decided to catch a train. There was a 6:38 southbound. I jumped on that one with seconds to spare. I fell asleep, and wound up riding it all the way down.

To Hakata.

SHUTTERSTOCK

AYUTTHAYA, THAILAND

Retribution

Later, we couldn't say we hadn't been warned. We most certainly had.

We were still a long way from Khaosan Road, Bangkok, winding our journey south through Thailand, when we ran into an emissary of that mecca for global backpackers and hitchhikers, Aussie's on their year-long "walkabouts," surfers from San Diego, and groups of Pakistani youth who traveled in bulk to keep costs low. He was the one who warned us.

One thing unified us all: intensely casual "backpacker" clothing, the kind that Thai tourist authorities did not want anyone wearing when visiting national historical sites like the Jade Buddha in Bangkok or Wat Chedi Luang in Chiang Mai. Signs warning us "travel rabble" against improper attire were everywhere at these hallowed sights; but enforcement was spotty at best.

A week prior, we had rented motorbikes and cruised, without helmets, of course, through the jungled ruins of the former Thai capitals of the Srivijayan Empire. The Thai and Burmese had clashed many times in history, particularly during the last thousand years. The Siamese capital city had moved up and down a roughly north-south line. We'd ride the train from one ancient town to the next, rent motorbikes for self-guided touring, and move by train again the next day. We ranged north to Sukothai, Phitsanulok, Lampang, and Chiang Mai. From there, we'd aimed to range as far north as we could by motorbike, to the Golden Triangle frontier town of Chiang Rai.

Yet there was still more Thailand north of us. We fueled up the bikes, and blazed a trail toward the Laotian border, over thin jungle roads ambulating through low passes in the hills until at last we crested a rise and gazed upon a great river, a wide and meandering blue-green swath. The end of our northward push, the Mekong.

Kids were swimming on the Thai side of the river, and for a brief moment, we pondered it. A swim. Across the Mekong, to set foot in Laos. It was a compelling proposition. "That river is pretty wide," I'd said.

"Looks kind of swift in the middle," added Jake.

Then we heard a familiar *thwhop-thwhop-thwhop* in the distance. It grew louder.

From beyond the river's bend, flying at tree top height above the water, a UH-1 Huey helicopter swept into view. The river, the jungle, and the chopper were a scene straight out of "Apocalypse Now." The machine passed nearly over our heads.

"Laotian Air Force?" pondered Jake. "I'm going to take a pass on that swim. You go ahead."

"Well," I said, "since that's just Laos over there, never mind. I kind of had my heart set on swimming to Cambodia." Which conversation I recount here with apologies to Francis Ford Coppola and Spalding Gray.

There's no more exhilarating way to explore an historic realm than to ride through it on a motor bike, risking life and limb in the process, absorbing bugs in one's teeth, but benefiting from the total freedom to go where and see what you want. In Thailand, our low-budget and self-actuated approach to sightseeing was a natural fit with the country's low-cost laissez-faire abundance of cheap vehicles for rent – no license needed, no questions asked. Helmets were never optional. There were none to be had.

In every town we visited, except Bangkok, we adopted this approach. In Bangkok, we relied on the professionals in their nimble traffic-beating three-wheeled tuk-tuks, which accounts for how we lived to tell of our journey.

After several days in the hilly frontier regions around Chiang Mai we were following the rails south through the ancient capitals, and were ready to check-into our next lodgment, a little traveler's motel in Ayutthaya. Our final "ancient capital" – next stop Bangkok, and back to the "cheap and cheerful" (as the Aussies would say) foreigner's ghetto of Khaosan Road.

Here in the motel lobby in Ayutthaya we met the one who warned us. "Aye, blokes," said a long-haired blond guy who could have passed for Peter Frampton, down to his British accent. "You might not want to stay here. Wish I hadn't."

He'd been on his way out as we entered. Beyond him was the hotel desk, behind which was the manager, a Thai man in middle years who squinted at us; he looked tall under the low, dark ceiling.

"Why?" asked Jake. "Bed bugs?"

The Frampton look-alike pointed a thumb back at the manager. "They bleedin' ripped me off. Me money, books, everythin' of value, except this." He held up his passport. "Went out for breakfast and when I come back, all me stuff was strewn about. They pilfered me music tapes, me Walkman." He turned to face the manager. "Me bleedin' *notebook*," he shouted. "Friggin' bogus, mates. Bogus. Yeah!" he shouted at the manager. "You bleedin' well know what *bogus* is, don't you?"

Mr. Frampton then wished us good luck and exited, carrying nothing but his passport.

So, again, we were warned. We'd been on the move in Asia for a year now, and had been circumspect with vital possessions. Everything critical went with us at all times – money, camera, passport. We were adherents of the "Command Bag" principle, which stipulates while traveling one never loses sight of their "nuclear football," the backpack or satchel that contains the key items for continuing the trip, and eventually getting home.

We were confident. We had no idea what really happened to Mr. Frampton's stuff, so we proceeded to check-in. Jake informed the manager. "Two beds. No bed bugs, please."

The manager said nothing. He took our Baht and gave us a key. Ayutthaya awaited, and we were eager to see it.

In Ayutthaya, we enjoyed one more day of riding tall in the saddle. Pockmarked palaces poked majestically out of the forest canopy, pale white curved monoliths surrounded by the constant chatter of monkeys, exotic birds and buzzing hordes of unseen insects, whose sound implied a mass of aggregated lifeform that was the stuff of nightmares; were it not so constant and pervasive. Instead, it served as background music to the adventure.

Ayutthaya, having inherited the role of capital city from Sukothai in the 1300s, had ruled Siam for 400 years. The ruined palaces and collapsed facades were courtesy of Burmese raiders, who had swarmed, besieged, and burned the great city in 1767. The next king of Siam moved the seat of power down the Chao Phraya River to the site of present day Bangkok, and there it has remained.

After nightfall, we dined on rapturous Thai stir fry at a roadside stall, and returned to our Ayutthaya hotel. We entered our room, dog tired, and ritualistically broke out our paperbacks. A few pages in, sleep crested like a tsunami, the type of sleep that hard travel and exposure to the wonders of life often sets upon the weary journeyer.

In the morning, sun glinted through the single high window of our room. I squeezed into the tiny bathroom, attended to diurnal business and a refreshing cold shower.

Jake, a practical character who'd learned to milk every last second of slumber during his U.S. Army years, leapt up when I emerged from the shower to conduct his business, and with our southbound train to Bangkok a few hours off, we went off to forage for breakfast

In the lobby, the clerk, apparently the manager's son, advised us. "Good breakfast, down the road that way," he informed us. "You very like."

We strolled five minutes in the indicated direction and found the restaurant. We did very like. If you've never enjoyed a traditional Thai breakfast, I recommend it. Anything you might order for lunch or dinner is generally also available at breakfast. I found this establishment's Moo Ping – pork skewers – to be sweet and spicy. A variety of fiery sauces made for high adventure dining, and glutinous rice served to salve excess spice that might otherwise inflame tongue and throat.

"Back to the slums tonight," Jake said, a forkful of food in his mouth, referring to Khaosan Road.

"Oh, it's not so bad," I said. The door to the restaurant opened and someone peeked in. I caught sight out of the corner of my eye. A small figure scanned and ducked out – fast.

"Was that the kid at the front desk?" I asked.

Jake's eyes narrowed. He was thinking what I was thinking.

"Doesn't matter," I said. "Even if Peter Frampton was straight up about being ripped off, there's nothing in our room worth a damn."

Jake wiped his mouth with the napkin, which was a toilet tissue-sized square of rough white paper. "True," he said, "Yet I don't take kindly to pilfering."

We finished up quickly, paid the bill, and exited into bright sunlight filtering through leafy coconut trees. Across the road, leaning on the handlebars of a bicycle, was the young hotel clerk. We saw him first, and waved. He didn't wave back; he hopped onto the pedals and bolted down the road, glancing over his shoulder at us twice.

"What," said Jake, "no courtesy wave? Let's double-time back."

"Relax, Jake. He's just a kid, there's probably nothing to be concerned about."

"There best not be, or we shall exact a high toll." The kid beat us back to the hotel, but not by more than a minute.

We threw open the hotel room door and I felt blood rising into my ears. "Well, now, this is nice!"

Stuff was everywhere. It was just like Mr. Frampton had described. Most of my clothes were on my bed. Jake's stuff was scattered. His duffel bag had been sliced asunder like a beluga whale at the hands of Captain Ahab, the work of his own pocket knife, which lay on the bed with the large cutting blade still open. Seems the kid had delivered warning of our impending return in the middle of the mayhem, and the pilferers had abandoned ship in a hurry.

"Damn it," I said. "This is bullshit. Let's go confront this band of thieves."

Jake, who'd seen a thing or two in parts of the world he wasn't at liberty to mention, held up his hand. "No," he said with calm. "Silent warning. Silent justice."

"What are you talking about?"

He showed me. It was mostly very familiar stuff. We'd both grown up with irritating siblings, so I understood the drill right away. And we'd done this stuff in college, after all.

We worked methodically, with another ninety minutes before our train would make its brief stop at Ayutthaya station, a ten minute stroll from here.

First, we sacrificed my collection of dead insects gathered on the trip, and laid them in my bed, carefully covering their corpses with the thick top-sheet. An arthropodal smorgasbord surprise awaited whoever next dealt with this bed.

We blocked the door with a heavy wooden nightstand. The room had a small kitchenette, and a closet with a broom and mop. We filled a large tin cooking pot with water, then hit upon inspiration. We dumped the water and did our best to fill it instead, shall we say, with personal metabolic waste fluids. Jake sucked down a few bottles of water; he intended to re-charge quickly. Then we wedged the pot up against the ceiling with the mop handle. Whoever pried open the door would be doused.

Jake is a Mormon, but he's not much of one. He consigned his St. Christopher medal by impaling it on the wall with my pocket-knife, all in the cause of "silent warning."

The big show was Jake's bed. He took clothes we intended to ditch before flying home in a week or so, along with crumpled newspapers and toilet rolls and created what appeared to be a human form under the top-sheet.

Then he whittled a sharp point on the toilet plunger handle, and thrust it into the "body." Given our desire to have it stand straight-up, we had to puncture the thin mattress and drive the stake into the bedsprings. Incidental damages, given the fully depreciated nature of the bedding. I had some catchup packets in my backpack from our one fast food visit on this trip, an A&W Root Beer in Kuala Lumpur, and we employed these around the "entry wound." By the looks, this dummy had been murdered in its sleep, stabbed to death with a plunger.

I'd inherited a partially consumed bottle of Mekong Whiskey, the national liquor of Thailand. It had been presented to me, as is, by an Aussie lass flying home the day we began our northbound train trip. "Mighty powerful stuff," she'd said. "No cooties!"

"Hmm. Bet I could use this to light the place on fire, were I so inclined," I informed Jake.

"Give me that," he said. "That's amateur thinking." He stepped into the toilet, opened the bottle, and somehow mustered a little more urine to spice up the whiskey. It was almost full, and still looked like whiskey.

"Good one," I granted. "Someone's gonna get pissed on that for sure."

Whoever next entered that room, after being doused with urine, would see a dead, bleeding body impaled in one bed, and dozens of freakishly large insects under the covers of the other. They would face St. Christopher, stabbed in the back, as it were. When they opened the kitchen cupboard a string of dental floss would yank out and dump a container of dried oatmeal flakes. The container held back the four plates and four bowls that were tilted on their side, and these would tumble and shatter on the tile floor.

We had a little more time, and had to get creative now. The dental floss was lain as trip wire in multiple locations, strung tightly to a cheap flower vase and the bed post, the shower curtain to the shower faucet, and so on. None of these were apt to hurt anyone. Still, I thought, a worthy effort.

Jake still had his pocket knife, and slit his thumb carefully. He squeezed enough blood to write "Silent warning, silent justice" and a crimson skull and crossbones on a sheet of spiral notebook paper. Then he consigned the knife by stabbing the note to the wall.

Satisfied with our thoroughness, we executed our escape, which was tricky with so many booby traps in place. Jake gave me a boost and I squeezed out the high window. He handed me the backpacks which landed with a plop on the foliage. I dropped to the ground. I stood to see that Jake was struggling a bit – that window was small – but he emerged, and landed with instincts instilled by the 101st Airborne, knees bent and a shallow roll onto his rump.

We were dusting ourselves off when we saw the bicycle kid staring at us.

"Sawadee Khrap," I shouted to him. "See you next time." Then we began strolling toward the train station. We could hear the kid shouting, no doubt reporting to his father that the *farang's* were making a suspicious escape.

"Shall we?" Jake suggested. We broke into a jog. Our train was still a few minutes off, but another southbound train was rolled in, and we jumped on it. At the first stop, we disembarked and then caught the Bangkok bound train.

"It would be great to bump into Mr. Frampton again," said Jake, "and inform him that justice has been served."

"Yes," I said. "This fine work of retribution would no doubt make Frampton come alive." For such a sappy play on a beloved album title, Jake said nothing. He just gave me a derisive sneer.

Silent warning.

EXPATRIOTISM

TIANMU, TAIWAN

Day One

It's remarkable how much my perspective on life was dislocated on that very first day in China, what with a near-death experience and all.

Purists will say, "No! Taiwan is not China!" and they are correct, now, today, somewhat. Much has changed, but in 1987 Taiwan was "China Plus" – China plus a burgeoning democracy, China plus a thirst to internationalize, China plus McDonalds, China plus a free press, and China plus super-charged economic growth.

Across the Strait of Formosa in Deng Xiao Ping's mainland China were none of those things, yet. Still, the language, culture, social behaviors, history, and approach to life were very much the same in Taiwan as in China.

On day one it was as if I'd walked into brain surgery. The doctor had opened up the hood, played with all the dials, been called away on emergency, and I'd been released into the world with my skull still wide open. Coincident with that feeling perhaps was that it was a rare cloudless day in Taipei. I felt the sunshine dazzling directly onto my cortex.

On that first full day in Taiwan, I was offered a

job, propositioned by a beautiful woman, hit by a bus, and converted to a new religion – all before 9:00am. By day's end, I would make numerous blunders, some of which may have been misdemeanors in this strange land. I went to bed that first night truly a changed man.

Few can claim to have been hit by a bus. Communication becomes tricky once one has been killed on impact. My encounter with a thirteen-ton Taipei city bus *did* inflict severe injury, from which I've never fully recovered.

After I strolled onto the noisy, bustling city street my first day in Asia, I waded upstream through a mass of loudly clamoring elementary school students. They looked like a hobbit army in their identical white shirts and blue shorts and skirts, each equipped with a uniform bright yellow backpack.

Open air food carts, sizzling with scallion cakes and stinky tofu, were clustered on street corners. The sights, smells, and sounds were dazzling to me. I wanted to learn all I could of this fascinating nation. Perhaps, I thought, I should explore Taoism or Confucianism, insofar as—

In that instant, I was struck by the bus. It hurt.

The bus was barely moving, and was one of several buses revving their engines in a bus station driveway. I had blocked the driveway by stopping to assess the wonders of Taipei city life at peak rush hour. The driver braked after his bus and my left shoulder tried to share space.

He probably couldn't believe that a gawking foreign pedestrian had failed to notice the advance of his lethal death mobile. I had the wind knocked from my lungs and had been pushed off the driveway into the busy street. My legs were fumbling to get underneath my body while drivers in fast moving cars and taxis were blasting their horns and crazily jockeying to avoid being the driver that put the coup d' grace to this crazed foreigner.

Somehow, through no grace of my own, I found my feet. I turned to face my would-be terminator, a thin, older gentleman wearing a black cap. He was gripping the wheel of his bus, and once again, nudging gently forward into traffic. I found this behavior unfathomable. Was he not going to jump out of his bus, run to my side, and render first aid? Or shout for immediate medical help?

No, he was not. He appeared to have places to go, and he was going to them right now. He had snarling, screaming traffic to intimidate. I could feel blood heating my ears, and my outrage stirred. I took a step back toward the driveway and my would-be assassin. I ignored the car screeching to my left, which was forced to stop as I advanced toward the wide, front glass of the bus.

The bus driver took notice, and he accelerated toward me to take advantage of the traffic break I'd just created. He was going to hit me, again!

A few years later, during the Tiananmen Square uprising, a truly brave, young man stopped the advance of a People's Liberation Army tank in the streets of Beijing. He blocked the behemoth armored vehicle, which tried to maneuver around him, then he ran over to block it again.

Luckily for me, I could not imagine such bravery. While defiance yet welled within, I am in honesty a world-class chicken at heart. I leapt to the right, and the front of the bus passed me a split-second later. Then with a wheeze of air brakes, it halted again, as the driver encountered more traffic. I was now staring directly at the driver through the side window, close enough that I could have yanked his shirt sleeve, and I aimed to do so. You try to kill me, fine; but I shall not be ignored!

He turned to face me, gave a little wave. He smiled. He nudged his bus forward, and again, I was imperiled. I jumped to the relative safety of the driveway, and watched him roar into traffic to the protests of vehicle horns. I watched the other four buses, driven by his comrades in arms, follow in his traffic-clearing wake, and roar one after the other in echelon onto the street. I watched them all drive away.

While believing my injuries were minor, there was no denying deep tissue damage. To my ego.

Just what did I think I was doing? I wondered, as I rubbed my injured left shoulder.

Had I quit my job in a top-flight aerospace company only to be flattened by a maniacal old man driving a bus?

Was it for this I had kissed good-bye a perfectly fine girlfriend, one who had assured me that she would *not* be waiting around for me to chase my own tail back to California?

Worst of all, had I surrendered the keys to my own shiny new vehicle, a jet black Toyota MR2, to a friend who, being a *true* friend, had promised to put spurs to my sleek sports machine on the mean streets of Los Angeles at every opportunity – only to make back page news in the Taiwan Times?

FOREIGN VISITOR *KILLED* IN BIZARRE SLOW-MOTION BUS ACCIDENT

SUICIDE - MENTAL ILLNESS SUSPECTED

Perhaps not.

As the morning throngs maneuvered the sidewalk around me, I began my immersion into my new religion, Taoism. Or Buddhism. Confucianism?

Anyway, they were all on my list of things to try during my visit to **Mysterious Asia**. I wondered why was I really here, if I could possibly stay, and what it all meant. I'd set foot in a country of people who spoke a legendarily difficult language in which I had no facility. In this new land, I was effectively deaf and mute until I could figure out some basic utterances.

Taiwan was in its 38th year of martial law, essentially in a cold war with the People's Republic of China. I had no job, no means of support, and I knew only one person, who'd just arrived himself a few weeks prior.

I stood there among the streaming masses of commuters. With $500 in traveler's checks I wasn't sure how to convert into currency, my persistence here was questionable. Realistically, my longevity in this **terra incognito** would be on the order of weeks, maybe days. I had always been the pickiest eater I'd ever met.

How long before I wasted away from hunger? I

patted my American-made tummy, reassuring myself that perhaps I could tough it out for a month or two after all. My one redeeming skill here was an aptitude for chopsticks. My father – a man so unhandy that he would call a plumber on Sunday rather than decode the mysterious technology of the toilet plunger – had granted me this one invaluable acumen.

He'd take my brothers and me into San Francisco's Chinatown. I'd have spare ribs and white rice, served with butter, of course. The waiters had politely obliged this strange behavior, but even then I harbored no illusions: the Chinese ate everything, by which I was shortly to learn meant *everything*. My repertoire had expanded to include Kung Pao Chicken a few years prior, and it was to this thin thread of hope I clung as I had bought my air ticket.

I continued my stroll. My newly acquired Zen Buddhist approach to life was paying off. While navel-gazing, brain open to the sunlight, I realized that I had completely ignored the many muttered curses, jostling elbows, and the briefcases slamming the backs of my knees.

Moments ago, I had been attacked by a bus, and my instinct had been to counter-attack. Now, I was at peace with the chaos, the noise, and the smokey air. In my first hours in this new land, I felt transported to a novel state of mind. Yet, something troubled me. I glanced at my watch.

It was nearly 8:45am, and I still hadn't had my first cup of coffee. I remembered that was why I had begun this saunter in the first place. Starvation would never have time to claim me if I could not fulfill this most critical task. My eyes roved up and down the street.

My friend and new roommate, Jake, was a Mormon, so I was on my own. He'd mentioned something about a donut place. Coffee is nearly as omnipresent today in Taiwan as it is in Seattle, but in 1987, it was available only at the Mister Donut shop in the foreign ghetto of northern Taipei, Tianmu.

Soon I would come to learn that there was, actually, one more place where coffee could be found – The American Consulate. McDonald's was so-called, because that's where you could find what few Americans were nearby in any Taiwanese town. A few years later, McDonalds announced a "200 Restaurants by Year 2000" target – which they breezed through -- and now have more than 400 sites in the Republic of China. When I first arrived, though, there was one per county.

"Hello, I would like to help you." The mellifluous voice drew me around to view its source.

A young woman, perhaps my age, dressed in a blue suit coat, black skirt, white blouse, and a black bow-tie. She wore a shy smile that framed almond eyes that glinted in the morning sun and radiated friendliness. Her long, black hair was thick with tresses. I wouldn't say she was drop-dead gorgeous. Doing so might mark me as superficial and susceptible to a lethal combination of charm and beauty. Maybe she was, maybe she wasn't.

Notwithstanding all that, my heart performed a small gallop up my esophagus making me stumble in asking, "Uh…Pardon?"

"I would like to help you," she said, in an accent that I can only characterize as cute. Or beguiling. Or perhaps fetching. Maybe adorable. "Are you lost?"

"No, no," I stammered. "And thank you. I'm

just looking for coffee."

"Drink coffee?" she asked, and raised her closed right hand like a cup to her mouth. "You want to drink coffee?"

"I *very* want to drink coffee," I said, to which she giggled. She checked her watch.

"You follow me," she said. "I show you Mister Donut." She strode in the direction I'd been heading before I was hit by the bus and discovered Zen Confucianism.

She knew! She would lead me to Mister Donut, the Promised Land, and my slow headachy death from caffeine deprivation would be narrowly averted. I smiled when she looked back and waved me on. A beautiful woman had approached me and was now leading me to a rare source of coffee.

I resolved right then and there that from this day forward, I would always adhere strictly to my new Jainist principles; they were clearly paying off.

That resolve did not flag one iota, even as I tripped on a sudden invisible increase in the sidewalk's altitude, and repeated my "bus impact dance" before regaining balance. My coffee goddess offered me some sound advice: "Be care-fff."

It was not the last time I would hear this. It was, in fact, the very first word of Chinglish I learned. I logged a mental note: one, always adhere to the ways of the Bodhisattva, and two, be care-fff at all times.

"Here," she said, a moment later. "We have arrivaled." It was an actual Mister Donut. "You drink coffee here."

Everything I previously said about not having true bravery and being a chicken-at-heart? Forget all that. At this moment, I demonstrated courage on a

Tiananmen Square scale. I asked her: "Would you like to join me for coffee? It would be my pleasure."

I was rewarded with her reaction, which was to hold her cupped hand in front of her mouth while she giggled. "No, thank you." She pointed to her watch. "I go to work now."

"Oh, OK." That made sense. She had by all appearances been on her way to work when she'd chanced onto the discombobulated foreigner who seemed lost but was in fact only lost in his new state of karma sutra type tranquility.

She covered and giggled. Again. "Would you like to teach me?"

What? What was this? Surely, she knew how to drink coffee…I opened my mouth without covering. No words issued forth from it. What did she mean? *Think!* I thought; *employ your Zoroastrian Asha pathways to logic out—*

"I would like you to teach me English." More giggles.

Of course! This was one very smart young woman. Somehow, her **chi** sensed within my **aura** that I had a Bachelor of Arts in English (with a minor in Technical Writing; check my CV for details).

I said, "I would very like…I mean, I would love to teach you English. What's your name?"

"Linda."

"No," I said, "I mean, what is your **real** name?"

"Linda," she repeated. "My Chinese name is Shu Mei."

"Shu Mei? Shu Mei. That's a lovely name, Shu Mei. My name is Tim."

"Dim. Nice to meet you, Dim" said Linda Shu Mei, and she extended her hand. We shook. She reached into her purse and pulled out a white card. "This is my *ming pian.*"

"Ah, your name card." She extended it to me with two hands, and I managed to accept it with two hands, and it was good that I did, so as to respect *Guan Yu*, the Chinese god of honor. Passing or receiving one-handed is inconsiderate. Also inconsiderate is not offering one's own *ming pian* in return, and I flustered to explain that I hadn't yet made my Chinese card.

"You just come to Taiwan?" she asked. "Are you Aussie?"

"No," I said, "I'm from California, and yes, I just arrived last night." I wanted to both learn and *use* my new Chinglish.

Shu Mei looked at her watch. "Oh!" She opened her purse, got a second *ming pian* out along with a pen. "You have telephone?" I did, and I'd written it down, just in case I got lost. I copied it onto her card, and wrote my name "D I M." My Chinglish name. She held her hand pinky down, thumb to ear. "I call you tonight, Dim. Talk about English teaching and price."

We exchanged bows, as is our Shinto custom here in Mysterious Asia. I went into Mister Donut and quickly attained a state of caffeinated nirvana.

The rest of the day, the very first full day in China, there were metaphysical incidents, there was fractious pushing and shoving, there were little old ladies I learned were called "Ah Mas" cutting me off in line at the store and the post office, and there was trying to buy a train ticket with no words for train, ticket, date, or time. The old me, the pre-bus collision me, would have been frustrated and tearing my hair out.

Ah, but that was before I'd discovered the ways of *Ganesha*. Linda Shu Mei did call me that first night, and she was all business. My first English student also taught me the power of negotiation, as practiced by the *kami Kuebiko*. She made me an offer I couldn't refuse. When I told Jake of the arrangement and the low billable rate to which I'd agreed, he had a philosophical observation to offer.

"There's a sucker born every minute," he'd said. "By which I mean, you."

He knew how to punch my buttons. Somehow, I restrained my inner *Shiva*, and assumed a Gandhi-like composure.

Later, I followed the way of *Chuangshen* and fell into a jet-lag induced spiritually-fueled state of slumber. It was the deep sleep of the dead, almost. I know for a fact it wasn't quite because the dead do not snore loudly enough to be awoken with late night blows to the head from their roommate's pillow.

CHUNG LI, TAIWAN

Have You Eaten?

"Well, have you? *Punk*?" I didn't know what to say to this Clint Eastwood juxtaposition. Jake knew damn well I hadn't eaten yet. Neither had he, and we both had to be hungry, it was nearly dinner time.

"*Hái méi yǒu*," I told him. Not yet. "*Punk*."

"Good use of Chinese," he said, "but wrong answer. It's exactly what I told my first English student at our initial tutoring session. And it was wrong to do so."

"How's that?" I asked.

"It's the culture," said Jake. "This guy, Chen, had greeted me with 'Have you eaten?' and I'd reflexively answered 'No, not yet.' He got very bothered about it, I sensed. Then he invited me to have dinner at his house after the lesson."

"Well, great job," I assured Jake. "There you are, stranger in a strange land, suddenly with a social invitation."

"Pay attention," chided Jake. "I'm teaching you something important. Two things, actually. First, the dinner invite ploy is a clever way to get an English lesson at a discount." He illustrated by underscoring the high rate of pay we could extract as language teachers versus the low cost of food. "Students will pick up the tab, but you'll yack with them for hours. In English, of course. Non-billable hours. But that, it turns out, was definitely not this."

"How so?" I inquired.

"Because, hailing someone with 'have you eaten?' in Chinese culture is the equivalent of 'how are you?' Meaning, it's not really a question, or if it is, there is only one polite answer. 'I'm fine.' Or, 'yes, I've eaten.'"

"Oh…" I said. "Oh yeah. So, you turned down the dinner invite."

"No," he corrected. "I accepted gladly. I was hungry, and wasn't going to turn away a free meal with a potential new friend, especially since I had no friends at all in this country. Hell, I didn't even have *enemies*. That's sad. Plus, he was a paying client. I didn't want to disappoint him. And, though I'd learned it in Chinese school, I kind of forgot the 'have you eaten?' bit being just a polite greeting."

"You *forgot*," I said, "or you *conveniently* forgot? Kind of a nitwit thing to do."

"Maybe," said Jake. "Once I accepted Chen's invite, he quickly came to grips with the fact that he was going to bring a foreign stranger into his wife's home without notice, and he was all smiles."

"Good job," I said. "Once again, the ugly American converts his lack of cultural awareness into a positive outcome."

"Not precisely," he countered. "After dinner, there was an incident."

"How's that?" I asked.

"They wouldn't let me leave," said Jake. "We'd finished up and I'd even given a few courtesy burps, which you know are interpreted very positively by the host—"

"You told me about the burping," I reminded him. "Twice."

"I stood to leave, and he said: '*Qǐng zuò!*' and made the sit-down now gesture. '*Qǐng zuò! Qǐng zuò!*' So I did."

"That's lesson one," I pointed out. "No one is going to let you leave their house until they have thoroughly begged you to stay. That's just the cultural ethos in China. If even little old me can figure that out, it can't be too hard."

Jake's brow was furrowed. He seemed to be in deep contemplation. "Yeah," he said after a pause, "maybe I was glad for the company." Then he smiled and added, "But it was getting late. I really wanted to go home, and just couldn't get an accurate read. They'd gone to lengths to accommodate me. Didn't want to be rude."

"At some point," I said, "you just got to shuffle out the door."

"Five more minutes, I was thinking. Then Mrs. Chen announced it was trash night."

"You helped her take the cans out?" I said. "Very sweet of you."

"I would have," Jake said. "But that's not how it works here. Remember the ice cream truck this morning?"

"I kept hearing it," I said. "But never saw it."

"You're a moron, you know."

I felt no umbrage for this insult. Jake's pattern was clear: he insulted me on a fully-calibrated scale, from dumb to dumbest: ignorant, foolish, numbskull, moron or idiot, in that order. This alerted me to the magnitude of the lesson he was about to impart. 'Moron' signaled a juicy lesson.

"That tinkly circus ice cream truck music," he said, "like we grew up with in California is not – here in Taiwan – the harbinger of a curmudgeonly senior selling Eskimo Pies. That music here issues from the trash truck. It heralds the once-a-week pick-up, and no man, woman nor child can afford to miss it, lest they be buried in their own solid detritus."

"That's culturally very confusing for me," I admitted. "Perhaps I *am* a moron."

"That's been established," said Jake. "But there's more to this lesson. Mrs. Chen had served an unexpected dinner guest on short notice – me – but she refused my offers to help with the trash. She waved me off, grabbed a big pail of kitchen waste, wrestled it onto the balcony, and poured it out. Five floors down to the sidewalk. One of the premier apartments in the building, they're perched right over the trash dump zone. The garbage collectors use pitchforks and shovels to toss it into the trucks."

"Gack," I opined. "That's got to change." A month later, it did. During the year I lived in Taiwan, it seemed almost *everything* changed, and all for the better.

Jake and I were pleasantly surprised the day the garbage crew serenaded us with their ice cream truck music, did their regular spade work scooping up the mountain of filth outside our apartment building, and right behind them a second truck cut loose a bright orange dumpster with big signs imploring folks to put their trash in it. Some did, though many continued to toss it haphazardly next to the dumpster. Within a few weeks, this behavior corrected. The "Refuse Rubicon" had been crossed, and soon the nation had cleaned up its act, and its notorious rat problem receded.

Jake continued his dinner time tale. "Even after his wife had cleared the table, washed the dishes, brought us a plate of fruit, removed the empty plates, and made the trash drop, Mr. Chen kept yacking. I resolved to exit. It was nearly eleven, and I was getting a vibe from the wife. A 'wore out the welcome' vibe."

"Oooh," I said, "that's not a good vibe."

"I rose to leave, and Mrs. Chen came out of the kitchen, and said, *chǐng zǒu* at me, kind of under her breath. Not very enthusiastic, but I knew she ruled the roost, and now *she* was insisting that I stay. I thought. So, I sat back down at the table."

"Very awkward," I said.

"No, worse than awkward. Now she and Chen were *both* standing, and I was sitting at their table. They were staring at me, giving me the 'what gives?' look."

"What was that about?" I asked.

"I didn't have a clue. It was very uncomfortable. Then Mrs. Chen turned on her husband and shouted at him. *Tā qǐng zǒu! Xiàn zài!*'"

"But you already *were* sitting," I pointed out. "And what the hell did she mean by 'right now?'"

"She was telling her husband to get this damn foreigner out of her house *now*," said Jake. "Near as I could tell."

"What?"

"My Chinese ear isn't very good," said Jake. "A

153

lot of stuff sounds like one thing but means another. Before, she'd mumbled *chǐng zǒu* as an observation that I was finally leaving. I mis-read it as *chǐng zuò,*' please sit down. They sound the same, kind of. Anyway, my first ever English student came over to the table and used his very limited English. 'OK, you go home now. *Chǐng zǒu!*'"

"Ouch!"

"So I jumped up and bolted toward the door while they both mumbled courtesies. I bowed and said *xiè xiè* many times." Jake sighed. "Have to say, that was the best dinner I'd had in months."

"Ah," I said. "An inelegant start of a beautiful friendship."

"Oh, hell no," said Jake. "Chen called me the next day. He was suddenly too busy for English lessons. He probably took a lot of shit from his wife after I left. Burned that bridge – poof!"

A lesson so stark, and so valuable, that even this moron was able to grasp it.

Have you eaten? Yes, I have. Thanks. And how are you?

TIANMU, TAIWAN

Bathtub Curve

Mr. Wang's chubby body sprawled full-length in the tub. He wore an ear-to-ear grin as he realized Jake and I were staring, wide-eyed, at his antics.

"*Kàn dào ma?*" he asked. "You see? Very big. Comfortable, neh? Neh. Now, see these stones?" The entire two-meter length of the tub was built of tiny multi-colored textured stones "Feel! Feel them!"

Reluctantly, Jake and I reached forward and rubbed the surface on the foot-end of the tub. "Wow," said Jake. "Rough texturing."

"Now, watch me," Mr. Wang said. He scooted his body up and down the length of the tub, the bare skin of his back rubbing against the bottom of the tub and those thousands of tiny rocks.

I found the scene slightly unnerving, despite the fact that Mr. Wang still retained his shorts for this demonstration and the bathtub was dry.

Mr. Wang's grin evolved into something primal, like the expression of ecstasy a dog wears when it's found exactly the right spot to scratch with its hind paw.

"Rawwwwooooo...." He said. I think.

"*Wo ming bai!*" Jake said. I get it. Satisfied, Mr. Wang attempted to rise out of the tub with Jake's assistance. Mr. Wang took his tank-top back and tossed it over his shoulder.

He next led us upstairs to the rooftop. Four stories above street level, there was no railing.

155

Multiple low wires traversed the space and there were a couple of plastic chairs for sitting and watching the wires swaying in the breeze while catching some ultraviolet light.

The entire home was, like many in Taiwan and China, vertical. The ground floor is for the family business, second floor for husband and wife, third for kids, and fourth for grandma and grandpa.

I approached the edge warily, and looked down at the teeming street and sidewalks.

"Here," said Mr. Wang. "Listen to music, read book. Smoke. Get away from wife." Mr. Wang's cherubic face burst into laughter. "OK, you like?"

"*Xǐ huan, xǐ huan,*" said Jake. "*Duō shǎo?*" We like it. How much?

The rent was remarkably cheap for 2,000 square feet in northern Taipei. The entryway stairs closed the deal for me. One wall had been painted by the previous tenant in honor of his photography studio, named "California." The wall said "Welcome to California." We dug in our pockets for the first month's rent and handed it over to Mr. Wang, who spouted more helpful tips on his way out.

Jake took a black marker from his backpack.

"Watch this," he said, and scrawled his own message. Henceforth, when we entered our new Taipei vertical apartment we'd be greeted by the message, "Welcome to California – Now Go Home!" a popular bumper sticker of the day.

We moved in immediately. Other than the huge suitcase of Jake's Chinese language books I'd brought, we had our backpacks. I'd honestly thought he'd be happy to have his language texts handy, but he'd quickly set me straight.

"This is the Republic of China," he explained.

"I know where we are," I rejoindered.

"I'm not sure you do," he jabbed. "These books are full of the script used on the mainland. It's the shortened communist version mandated by Mao Tse Tung. Being soldiers, we were trained in the script used by our potential adversary. The script used here in Taiwan classical, and correct."

"Got it," I said. "Though I don't see China as a nemesis. I'd like to visit there. In the meantime, I'm loving life here in Taiwan."

"You just got here," said Jake. "You're still in the love-at-first-sight phase. I'm ahead of you by a month, and I'm already starting to see what the expats around here have told me."

"What's that?"

"They call it….oh, that's funny. How appropriate after Mr. Wang's bathtub demonstration. Ha!"

"Lost me," I said.

"They call it," said Jake, "the 'Expatriate Bathtub Curve' and it applies to anyone who lives in a new country. It's a sort of universal law of international relocation. Your first weeks or months are fabulous. Everything is great, exciting, different. It's better than home, and you wonder why your country can't be like this. The novelty of food, people, culture and customs is entertaining. You're on a high, like an extended sugar rush."

"Then," he continued, "little things start to eat at you. Things like no respect for queueing, the ubiquitous practice of public spitting, and people pushing past you to board the train. About the six-month point, you wake up one day and can't stand the place – the people are annoying, and their strange, uncivilized behaviors frustrate the heck out of your daily existence."

"Really?" I said. "I guess I'm still in the honeymoon phase."

"Yes," said Jake, "and good luck to us both staying there. The good news is, they say, about a year in you'll come to appreciate the good, the bad, the different. You slide down one end of the bathtub, hit bottom, and slowly rise back to some kind of equilibrium."

I would soon learn all this was true. The universe is not predictable, but there are some constants – speed of light, force of gravity, and the Expatriate Bathtub Curve.

Hunger called. We made our way onto the bustling evening sidewalk in search of food. I was still a little fuzzy on the difference between the languages.

"Spoken Mandarin," said Jake, "is almost identical here and on the mainland." He paused as we were split up by a large gaggle of evening shoppers coming the other direction. We continued upstream, toward the American Veterans club, which Jake assured would serve a taste of home for dinner.

"The differences," he continued, "are trivial inflections, but the writing...what a mess!"

"How so?" I asked, just as I tripped yet again on a sudden rise in the sidewalk, and barely kept my footing. "Dammit! I keep doing that."

"Oh, you'll get used to it. Every business essentially was built-to-suit, at slightly different levels, whatever made sense and optimized the land. If you're not watching, you're going to be tripping with regularity."

"OK, great," I said. "Now what's the difference between all these versions of Chinese?"

Jake turned to face me, mid-stride. "You really want to know?"

Then he, too, tripped, and recovered only after a drunken sailor walk of bouncing off a storefront window and finally grabbing a cement pillar. "Dammit to hell!"

I laughed. "Not the language of a good Mormon."

"There's the club. Let's get a beer. Ginger beer, that is. I'll tell you all about Chinese language over beer."

This, more or less, is what he told me.

SPRECIAL FEATURE !!!

Chinese-In-a-Box

Shopping for a new language? Why not try Mandarin Chinese?

There is an ancient Chinese idiom that can be interpreted: "Fear not Heaven, fear not Earth; fear only the foreign devil who can speak Chinese." As someone not born to the language, who has endeavored to learn it, I can assure any such concerned members of the Middle Kingdom that there is nothing much to fear.

So, you're a stubborn one. That's good, in that I will now show *you* the *best* way to learn Chinese, and I'll give you some options, and a tool-kit that will make it all so easy.

If you can arrange it, be born into a Chinese speaking family. If that ship has sailed, next, get immersion therapy via two years of strict missionary duty courtesy of the Latter Day Saints. If that is not your cup of tea (in that, perhaps, you wish to be permitted to *drink* tea), then next up: go live in China or Taiwan and don't speak anything *but* Chinese. Voila, in two to five years, if you look foreign enough, you may even become a minor tv celebrity on local game shows.

If none of the above suit you, fret not. I have

laid-out a simple process that I call "Chinese-In-a-Box" that's guaranteed (when gently soaked in years of sweat, toil, and hard work) to result in Chinese fluency.

A few things first. Know that there are many dialects of Chinese, all stemming from one common written language – until recently, at least. From the 38 provinces and regions of China come a dizzying array of patois, including Cantonese, Hakka, Shanghainese, and Hunanese, and another 76 dialects. Linguists say many of these dialects are further apart than French is from English – effectively not the same language. Perhaps it's more accurate to say they seem entirely unrelated.

In the past, this was a real problem. Chinese people would meet each other somewhere in or out of China, and not be able to communicate. A Cantonese speaker and a Shanghainese speaker would perceive the other as speaking in tongues, and revert to German or Spanish. Now, not so much, as the universal lingua franca in China is Mandarin. One dialect to rule them all. All you need is Mandarin. These days, when you say "I speak Chinese" you're saying "I speak Mandarin."

The unifying element of Chinese, the written characters, consists of 46,964 symbols. These are not phonetic letters in the sense of western languages, but closer to what linguists call morphemes – either simple or complex – units of meaning which derive from ancient drawings. All these characters can be built using combinations of just 214 radicals, or "strokes." Knowledge of about 2,000 to 5,000 of the traditional characters is necessary to be "newspaper" literate. By studying the 214 radicals, and learning to read and write a few thousand characters, a student can be literate in Chinese. And not just one dialect of Chinese, but *all* dialects – as the written language is truly common and essentially unchanged between all the many different Chinese dialects.

However…At some point in his long and disruptive rule, probably in a moment of boredom, Mao Tse Dong, convinced that he had not inflicted sufficient inconvenience on his people, decided that written Chinese was too complicated. While Mao championed the use of Mandarin as the national language, he also introduced the nuisance of a "simplified" character set. Simpler, perhaps, but adding an extra 6,500 characters. If you had worked hard and learned just the few thousand "newspaper" characters, your work was now suddenly just beginning.

The new "simplified" characters are abbreviated, requiring fewer strokes. So, that's something. They're supposed to look similar to the original characters, but in my humble assessment, not so much. They also added 49 new radicals, so the 214 basic building blocks became 263.

All this came about after tens of millions of Chinese no longer lived under the Chairman's tender jurisdiction – the populations of Taiwan, Singapore, and the millions in the global Chinese diaspora living around the world – and they tend to ignore these short characters. The short form has added a tremendous overlay of challenge for those who seek to read and write Chinese. So, thanks a lot for that, Mr. Chairman.

Remembering that there are many different dialects of Chinese, and you've wisely chosen

Mandarin, and it is a single written language give or take; and further, that we live in the digital age where thousands of characters can be read and written easily with the aid of your digital assistant, written Chinese takes on less importance. Speaking and hearing is the true objective of most folks studying a new language.

The next thing to know is that spoken Chinese is tonal. Tonal languages harness the inflection imparted by the speaker as a key portion of the meaning of each word. Speak the correct tone when saying the word for "horse" or you may well be heard to say the word "mother." Or "rope." Or "What?" Hearing the tones correctly is also important, but context makes interpretation easier.

Speakers of Romance Languages (English, Dutch, Italian, etc) are familiar with tones. We also use them, the difference being that our tones tend to impart emphasis or emotion, and they tend to inflect a phrase, as opposed to individual words. English uses a rising tone at the end of a sentence to indicate we're asking a question. Is that why our tone goes up at the end of a question? It is. Does it work that way in Chinese? It does not.

In Chinese, questions are indicated by what are called "interrogative" words placed at the end of the sentence. Think of the now little used language of the telegram.

HAS THE SHIP SAILED YET QUESTION
YES THE SHIP HAS SAILED STOP

Chinese has abbreviated single syllable morphemes that can be applied at the end of a sentence to indicate to the listener that the sentence is a question, command, observation, or exclamation.

Tonal languages deliver the advantage of maximizing differentiated meanings on fewer root sounds, or phonemes. One phoneme (akin to a syllable) can deliver multiple meanings, based on the tone used to deliver it. Chinese is not alone in operating this way – Thai, Vietnamese, and Punjabi are other examples.

Some Chinese dialects use up to eight tones. If you want to learn those dialects, I wish you a lot of luck. Mandarin Chinese has but four tones, as we shall see. Some will claim there are five, perhaps because they enjoy hair-splitting. There is a neutral tone, which is no tone at all, and isn't used to inflect meaning.

Now, before I unveil your "Chinese-In-a-Box" kit, let's underscore some guidelines that will abet your learning process:

1. Refuse Pronunciation "Training Wheels." Never try to learn Chinese pronunciation by reading Romanized characters. Yes, I'm talking about *you* Pinyin and *you* Wade-Giles. These "systems" are punji-stick infested pits; if you fall into one, it will hurt and send you to a dark pronunciation prison, where you'll forever be mangling the language. These cretinous crutches hobble you by attempting to redefine symbols that you *already know* (the alphabet) and assign *different* (uniquely Chinese) pronunciations to them.

That's just plain confusing. The Pinyin symbol purported to represent a "ch" sound is given as "j". Except, sometimes the pinyin for the "ch" sound is not given as "j", rather it is indicated by "q". Pinyin can help the non-speaker sound out some things, but as a tool for learning it is a disaster. A disaster wrapped in a calamity, folded into a cataclysm. Quantum leaps better to use some fresh symbols untainted by our phonetic prejudices to learn the correct Chinese sounds.

Accordingly, your "Chinese-in-a-box" kit includes 37 symbols that were developed by smart people in China expressly for teaching correct Chinese pronunciation. It's called: ㄅㄆㄇㄈ (pronounced as the starting sound of these letters – B, P, M, F, aspirated as "Buhhhh, Puhhhh, Muhhhh, Fuhhhh"). Yes, it's 37 more new characters you must learn – only 37, not 3700 – but once you do, it's possible to visualize and *read* aloud all Chinese through its use. Mastery of ㄅㄆㄇㄈ (Buhh, Puhh, Muhh, Fuhh) means that you will have learned to correctly articulate all the phonemes of the Chinese language – a feat that will impress the daylights out of any native speaker.

Get the 37 sounds of Chinese right at the start, and you will quickly be a Mandarin rock star. No exaggeration.

2. **May the Tones Be With You**. They perhaps sound like the scariest challenge, but let's just see about that. First, there're only four: 1 – high; 2- rising; 3 – falling then rising; 4 – falling. They are symbolized like this:

mā	má	mǎ	mà
Ma-1	Ma-2	Ma-3	Ma-4
High	Rising	Fall-Rise	Falling

The best way to learn the tones is by listening and repeating, with feedback from a native Chinese speaker (tapes and YouTube are fine, but be sure to get feedback, too). Know that memorizing words in Chinese also means memorizing the tone. My English speaking brain was not wired for this, but the wiring adapts quickly.

Some find it easy to remember the tone as a number (1 through 4) while others just have the tone embedded in their "ear" without recourse to number or symbol. Either way, this will start to happen in a few weeks or maybe a month. Persistent patience, please.

It's ok to also start studying Chinese characters (traditional, non-Maoist, real characters), whipping through flashcards, and practicing calligraphy. But the proper way to learn Chinese (or any language) is the same way you learned your native tongue as a kid. Command of the spoken word is the linguistic high-ground; once you've seized a piece of that you're poised for greater conquests including the written characters. Try combining characters and tones on flash cards, like this:

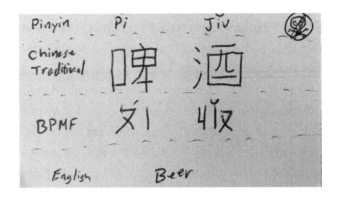

Master the four tones. Those who become fluent in the language without the tones are stuck in a flat quagmire – they will speak in a manner that most Chinese speakers will politely deem "cute" – even though they really mean "bizarre."

3. **Consider Firing Your Chinese Teacher**. If you decide to enlist the aid of a real, live Chinese language teacher, that's great, but you will need to choose wisely. If you've already got a teacher and you recognize an issue, don't be shy about summarily dismissing him or her and upgrade. Reasons for termination may include:

a. **Teacher can't speak Chinese**. Remember, you want Mandarin, and if your teacher is not a native or classically trained Mandarin speaker, you may go astray. There are famously 1.4 billion Chinese in the world, but many did not grow up speaking Mandarin as their first tongue. So unless you happen to live in Beijing, Taipei, or Monterey Park, California, the teacher you first choose may need to be vetted.

b. **Teacher can't teach**. Perhaps you found your Chinese teacher among friends or acquaintances who happen be ethnic Chinese, and even if you manage to get a native (or well-practiced) Mandarin speaker, chances are this poor victim is not a trained professional educator. If your instructor isn't catering to your needs (speaks too fast, loses patience, or particularly if he or she happens to be your spouse), then gently rotate personnel until you get someone who can adapt to your educational needs. (No, divorce is not necessary, and my legal team insists I state this clearly by way of example: if you're Wayne in Wayne's World, hire a teacher to teach you Mandarin and be nice to your lovely Cantonese beau. Indemnification complete).

4. Use It or Lose It. It's ok to annoy your Chinese waitstaff (up to a point), but if you don't have people you can practice with on a continuing basis then develop an interest in Chinese popular music and watch movies. Again, caution is required. CAUTION: do not lightly indulge in the musical form known as "Canto-pop" – not only is this Cantonese, it's also swooning bubblegum music, sticky stuff, high risk of "ear worms." Listen to Coco Lee, a sort of Chinese Celine Dion collides with Britney Spears. For movies, start with Jackie Chan's films dubbed in Mandarin – make sure you don't get the Cantonese, since most of the early ones were originally filmed in that much trickier and nonstandard dialect. Watch CCTV. No, it won't turn you into a Mao-jacket wearing communist, you silly person.

5. Be Persistent. While studying Chinese, feelings of stupidity are common. The learning curve seems insurmountable. What you don't know is that the process will snowball and accelerate. Speak and don't ever be shy. All languages are learned this way. As kids we say the darndest things and just keep learning. That's what you want to do. Learn more of Chinese culture, and you'll be reinforced and rewarded.   Pick-up some of the many colorful idioms: "Kill one to warn 100" (useful for mafia kingpins and lazy dictators).   "If you choose to ride the tiger you may find it difficult to climb down" (admonition to thrill-seekers).   And my favorite, "When drinking with an old friend 1,000 glasses are too few." There are plenty more.

These guidelines will serve you well. Remind yourself that spoken Chinese is the most used language in the world (followed by English, Spanish, Hindi and Arabic).   Over a billion people communicate with it every day, in China and globally. Summarizing the features and benefits:

1. Communicate directly with at least 1.4 billion more people
2. Chinese is the up and coming language for business in the 21st century

3. It's rich, complex, endlessly fascinating
4. For those who paint, draw, or doodle, practicing the written language is a source of artful joy
5. Learning the language will inevitably expose you to Chinese history, culture, cuisine and philosophy
6. Did I mention Chinese food? Did I *need* to mention it?
7. Imagine the joy of traveling in China using your newly-developed language skills, and the instant friendships you'll spark
8. Politics being what they are, your Chinese ability can open up new career opportunities, particularly if you also possess people skills, diplomacy, and what are innocuously referred to as "spy-craft" skills. Just for your information.

And now, at long last, what you've been waiting for, my patent-pending simple roadmap to Chinese success called "Chinese-In-a-Box." Got it? Then go ahead, open it, and follow these simple steps:

Step 1 – Open your box; really, go ahead, it's ok

Step 2 – Discard, in an environmentally friendly way, the packing peanuts, Chairman Mao's 6,500 short-form characters including the 49 new Maoist radicals (pardon the expression), and all Chinese dialects except Mandarin. In the unlikely event your box was incorrectly packed with Pinyin or Wade-Giles, use the included disposable gloves to pick these up and flush them immediately down the toilet. Scrub hands.

Step 3 – Retain the 5,000 "newspaper" characters for possible future use, and at your option you may dispose of the remaining 42,000 more arcane and seldom-used characters.

Step 4 – Make flashcards for the 37 ㄅ ㄆ ㄇ ㄈ ("Buhh Puhh Muhh Fuhh") characters, and learn how to correctly pronounce them. These lessons are easily found on Youtube (check a few to ensure you're hearing them consistently; consult a native speaker from time-to-time).

Step 5 – Start learning. Use Rosetta Stone or other language software with automated feedback, a native Mandarin tutor or class instructor, tapes, flashcards for help with tone and character memorization, online lessons, etc.

Step 6 – Speak and listen. Don't be shy about deploying your language skills at restaurants, with friends, family, and associates who speak the language. When conditions permit, contemplate a trip to Taiwan or China.

Four out of five linguists recommend choosing Chinese as your new language. With apologies to Hungarian speakers, struggling like mad to learn that tongue might be a fine hobby. Maybe there's a "Hungarian-In-a-Box" out there (compare pricing with Chinese-In-a-Box, which you got FREE as a bonus for reading this story).

So for those with ambition to learn a language, who travel, plan to do business sometime during the 21st century, or who just want a tool for social interaction with a billion more people, Chinese is where it's at.

TIANMU, TAIWAN

Language Skills

"You called her a what?" I asked.

"I'm not sure," said Jake. "But I think so. She'll never forgive me."

This is just great, I thought. Jake was the only person I knew well in this country. He was much further along studying Chinese than I, and he had just mortally offended nearly the only other person I knew, beyond my first language student, Linda Shu Mei.

Perhaps I *had already* offended her? If Jake could fumble the social football so easily in this culture, I was doomed. I might as well catch the next plane back to California. It was ironic that the trouble had started with a lecture by Jake on the treacherous nature of the Chinese language.

"And that, my friend," he had said, "is why Chinese is a bit challenging."

"You mean, as opposed to English?"

At that moment, the waitress at the American Veterans club in Taipei came by our table, saw our drinks were still half full, and without hesitation swept the gown of her blue evening dress aside and slid into

173

our semi-circular booth next to Jake.

"Do you mind?" she asked, in English.

We certainly did not. Nor should her boss, as the place was empty aside from our table and an older gentleman nursing a tall drink with a red umbrella poking out of it. The DJ, Reggie, was African American and spoke with a Cajun accent. The music was nice, contemporary 1980s hits, and the volume just right – you felt the vibe, yet could still carry on a conversation.

"I'm Cherry," said the waitress, who reached across the table to shake our hands. "Are you guys from California?"

"Wow," I said, "how did you know?"

"I've worked here a year," she laughed. "It's an all-American clientele. How's my English?"

"*Fēi cháng hǎo*!" said Jake. "Super good."

"Better than your Chinese," she giggled. "But you'll learn."

Jake looked annoyed. "I studied twelve months at Defense Language Institute in California."

"Oh, then you can speak quite a lot," she said. "That's great."

"*Xie xie, nǐ tài kè qi,*" he said. Thanks, you're too kind.

Cherry laughed. "It's funny. You're young, but you speak Chinese like my grandfather. Your teacher was old?"

"In his eighties."

We chatted for a few minutes. Reggie queued up Madonna's "Holiday" and did a neat trick blending it with a song, partially in Dutch, that I'd never heard before nor since, but never forgot. "We are going on a summer holiday, and if you want to go, yo, Sven!

We're going to London and New York City, and we'll take a little piece of Amsterdam...*right!*"

Reggie dragged and pulled on the spinning disks of the two vinyl records and made them merge and meld from one song back into the other. A fabulous performance, just for the few of us.

Before the song finished, Cherry rose and disappeared, and soon came back with a tray of drinks. She had one for the only other customer, a refill each for Jake and me, and a drink of her own.

She rejoined us, lifted her glass, and said "*So-yi!*" Then she tapped the bottom of her glass on the table top. We did likewise and sipped in unison. Jake bent Cherry's ear with tales of his six years in the U.S. Army, which had just ended with his completion of Chinese language school.

"So I came here to Taiwan," he told her, "to build my Chinese."

"Good for you," she praised him. "It's your chance to fix your pronunciation. What about you?"

"I'm here," I said, then paused. "It seemed like a good idea when he suggested it." I pointed to Jake. "It still does."

"You guys are real adventurers," she said. "I think you'll do well."

"Thanks," said Jake. "It's helpful to have a gracious hostess like you to guide us."

At that instant, time stood still. Cherry's smile froze. Something in her eyes changed. A great sheet of ice descended from above. The warmth on her face had become glacial cold. I felt it to the core. The few seconds felt like an unhappy hour. Then, she stood suddenly, straightened her blue dress, and left the table without a word.

175

"What did you say?" I asked.

Jake was as puzzled as I was. "Something wrong. I think I really offended her."

He had. We figured it out quickly. "Frigging horror freak show," Jake emphasized by way of self-flagellation. "I can't believe I said that."

"You didn't know," I assured him. "I didn't know. Now we both know." The English word 'hostess' implied something very different in Taiwan. In California, a host or hostess was the person who "hosted" guests. Here, as in Japan, "hostess" often meant a woman entertainer who not only hosted but could offer 'additional services'.

Without knowing it, Jake had called her a prostitute.

His expression was stricken. I'd never seen that look on him.

The song ended, and the room was silent. Reggie surveyed the still mostly empty club. He glanced at our sorry faces, picked up the microphone, and cleared his throat. "Check it out – candy store without no candy."

That triggered Jake to action. He slid out of the booth without a word and went through the kitchen door after our previously friendly waitress. He was gone quite a while. Reggie ran through a few more numbers, during which a couple entered and sat near the stage. Then a group of three, apparently also American veterans. The place was showing signs of life.

At long last, Jake returned to the table, a grin on his face. "She will never forgive me. Not ever, but I did the right thing. I explained that I'm an idiot. I begged her forgiveness. I got down on one knee and apologized."

Cherry came flying out of the kitchen door and brandished a smile for the new arrivals, and took their drink orders. She didn't even look in our direction.

Jake stood and extracted a large wad of New Taiwan Dollars (NTD). He counted out what had to be far in excess of our tab and left it on the table. "Best bet now is skedaddle." We did.

Jake was quickly proven wrong. About the forgiveness thing, at least. When we returned a few days later, Cherry sat with us to chat again, as if nothing had happened. We became regulars, and she introduced us to others on the staff. We started dropping by for a bite to eat or a drink almost every night.

A few weeks later, after we'd both lunched elsewhere, we packed it in early and didn't visit the club. Something wasn't sitting right. By morning, I was soaked in my own sweat, fevered and nauseous. There was no way I would be teaching. I stumbled downstairs to check on Jake. He looked like he'd been bitten by the same zombie that got me.

We managed to make some tea, work the phone to report in sick to our various teaching gigs, and then collapsed.

Two days went by, and we didn't leave the apartment. My head was a lead balloon, it was all I could manage to scrounge hot water and tea to avoid total dehydration. Time stood still. The world went by without us.

At midnight of the third day, my head began to pound loudly. I stirred in bed, sat up, and saw it was just after midnight. The pounding repeated, more fierce and more real. Someone was banging on our door. Jake and I stumbled downstairs. He reached the door first.

There stood Cherry and two other waitresses from the club, apparently just off-duty. "What's wrong with you guys?" she asked. "You look sick." They entered, and took control. Cherry fixed us tea while the others ran down the street for medicine. They were back in minutes.

"Take this," one said.

"How?" I asked, looking at a torn half newspaper she'd rolled into a cone, which now contained an intensely yellow powder.

"Like this," she demonstrated. Mouth open, head back, she made a pouring motion with the paper cone. "Then drink." She handed me a canned soda with a straw. I did as instructed.

After a few coughs, I managed to suck down the powdery preparation with a few swigs of cold soda. Then I burped.

"*Duì bu qǐ!*" I said.

The women laughed. They laughed even harder when Jake emitted the longest uninterrupted subterranean belch I'd ever witnessed. He finished it off and yawned.

"That's powerful stuff," he said.

He wasn't kidding. My vision was clearing and my head was no longer throbbing. In minutes I was standing, stretching, breathing deeply. "I'm hungry," I said.

"You are now fine," said Cherry. "Eat, get your strength back."

"Wait a minute," said Jake. "Did you just save our lives? We were really sick. What is this magic powder?"

"Not magic," she corrected. "Just Chinese herbal remedy." None of them would accept credit for saving our lives, yet that's exactly what they'd done.

The next night, we were back at the club. A week after that, Jake and Cherry became something of an item and began dating.

Language is a complex and difficult thing to master. Chinese for sure. This incident taught me that English – our native tongue – was more than challenging enough for numbskulls like us.

TIANMU, TAIWAN

Fortune Cookie

While Tianmu may have been the "Foreigner's Ghetto" of Taipei, most had left with the U.S. armed forces pull out in the 1970s. There were vanishing few foreigners to be found there in 1987. Jake, having arrived in country several weeks ahead of me, now seemed to know them all.

"We're going to meet Kimi-Toshi for lunch," he informed me on my third day. When we rendezvoused at the restaurant after a brisk walk from our pad, I was surprised to find that Kimi-Toshi was a blond, blue-eyed male.

"Jake," I whispered after we'd met and were following Kimi to our table, "I thought he would be Japanese. And female."

"Shh!" he admonished me. "He's Belgian. Don't piss him off." As regards this latter admonition, he had a good point. While not Japanese, Kimi was built like a Sumo wrestler, with an important difference: it was all muscle.

We sat. The waitress gave us three menus. I could not interpret mine at even the most rudimentary level, as they bore no English and no photos.

Kimi barked something harsh sounding at the waitress, who fetched a steaming pot of tea and three small, white cups. Pre-set on the table were three upside down rice bowls and three sets of paper-wrapped wooden chopsticks. He turned over his rice bowl next to the cups, made an exhibition of pouring hot tea into each of the three cups, and rinsing and pouring the residue into the bowl.

He then filled each cup with steaming oolong and shoved them out to Jake and I. He took our rice bowls, and swirled hot tea in those. He shouted at the waitress, who drained the rice bowls into a big noodle bowl that she'd just bussed at a nearby table. And this is how it was and still is in much of China. Folks make darn sure their cups and bowls are sterile at restaurants, and no restauranteurs ever take offense. They do the same thing.

Kimi-Toshi looked up at me. "What do you do here?"

Jake chimed in. "He just arrived from California. He's trying to adapt."

Kimi nodded. "Good luck to you." Then he turned to the waitress, who was now chatting near the kitchen door with another waitress. "*Xiǎo jiě*!" he shouted. When he got no reaction, he pounded the table with his meaty fist, provoking a sonorous rattle of tea cups. "*Xiǎo jiě*!!"

She broke off her conversation, sidled up to our table. "*Yào shén me?*" Literally, what do you want?

Kimi jabbed at his menu. "*Nà gè!*" he shouted. "*Nà gè, liǎng gè!*" Two of that. It occurred to me then, in the early days of my Chinese lessons, that this word could be subjected to misunderstanding, in so far as it sounded – much like the now little used English word "niggardly" – a little too much like something it most definitely wasn't. And so it has.

"*Nà gè*" means "that to which I am pointing" in Chinese, and "niggardly" – in English – means "stingy" and derives from an old Norse word which meant "poor." English is full of excellent surrogate terms for "stingy" but Chinese really does kind of depend on "*Nà gè.*" The good news: cross-cultural awareness awaits.

The waitress nodded and scrawled. Kimi was a regular here, and he always ordered the same thing, times two. He was, after all, a very big guy. Then Jake ordered. I had trained for this moment. I was ready.

The waitress turned to me.

I gave her a smile, not just to appear friendly, but also to cushion the damage I would now inflict on her native language. "*Gōng bǎo jī dīng,*" I said. To my surprise, she repeated it – with corrective phonetics, of course – and walked away.

"So, Kimi," I asked. "how long have you lived in Taiwan?"

The blond Belgian was lifting his fist to his mouth; inside the fist, I surmised, must be his teacup. He made a snorting sound, put the cup back down.

"Too long. Five years. Yah. Five years. Now, I take a shit." He stood abruptly and lumbered toward the back of the restaurant where a small sign posted above a door showed this:

"Jake," I said, "where did you find this guy?"

"Right here. I came in for lunch the day after I landed, and he was sitting at this table. He waved me over, invited me to join him. He's pleasant enough."

"OK," I said.

"But you should know, his Chinese sucks. He's functionally mute here. Plus, he has a bad temper. Careful with the questions. He triggers easily."

"OK," I said.

"No, really," said Jake. "He just got out of prison. He was there for two weeks."

"Taiwanese prison?"

"Hey, nobody in the slammer dared mess with him. Would you?"

"Oh, hell no," I offered. "What'd he do to end up in Chinese jail?"

"He slapped his girlfriend. Her dad is a county supervisor. But it's all good now. They made up, and the dad even managed to get him sprung a bit early. Shh, here he comes."

And in this manner, I began to suspect that Taiwan was a new frontier, and not just for people like Jake and I, who wanted to learn Chinese and – both of us considering MBA programs at some point – explore business opportunities. But also for the dispossessed, the misfits finding only unhappy niches back home in Europe, Australia, Japan, and America.

Lunch came on. The waitress placed the steaming bowl under my nose. I took a deep whiff and was plunged into a coughing spasm from the nearly toxic levels of pepper that tipped the Scoville Scale toward the red zone.

Kung Pao Chicken (宫 保 雞 丁, *gōng bǎo jī dīng*) is now the number one go-to dish for Americanized Chinese food. Ordering Kung Pao is like saying, "I'll have the burger."

Still, don't imagine that Kung Pao Chicken is exclusively a dish of Yankee re-engineering; it's a genuine Chinese creation from Sichuan Province, the certified spiciest province in the Middle Kingdom. It's active ingredient: Sichuan Peppercorns. These "black flavor modules" – as they are aptly described by a friend of mine – comprised the vast majority of the dish by volume. *Hěn là!* Muy caliente.

Kung Pao Chicken originated centuries ago, but was named and popularized in the 19th century after Ding Baozhen, a governor of Sichuan. Ding (丁) derives from Ding's name and is also a pun, since Ding describes the diced and cubed nature of the chicken meat. The rest is an extraction from Ding's title as governor, Gong Bao (宫 保).

My bowl served up a generous portion, and aside from the extreme density of black flavor modules and consequent extreme spice, it was much the same dish I'd get from my favorite Chinese lunch spot in California; although back home they chopped the chicken into cubes *after* removing the bones.

Details. Narrowly avoiding a chipped molar in this discovery, I learned to gnaw gently around the bone shards and remove them from my mouth with chopsticks. In a year of dining in Taiwan, I suffered no choking incidents.

Spicy food makes me sweat and my sinuses run. To lessen the deluge, the trick is to dilute the Kung Pao spice explosion with quantities of ultra-glutinous white rice, and quarts of oolong tea. Kimi loudly motivated the waitress to keep the teapot full and the rice coming. I'd brought a packet of tissues, having learned that napkins and toilet paper were very much a hit-and-miss proposition, and nearly exhausted my supply battling the nasal effluent generated by the onslaught of fiery chili.

While we ate, Kimi grumbled in broken English about how everything in Taiwan sucked, but that it was much better than Belgium. "Belgium is hell on Earth," he explained. "People are stupid there, the government is stupid, it's all stupid." Jake went out on a limb and asked him if he was working.

"Work is for suckers and Frenchmen," explained Kimi. Jake deftly changed topics. It was a tasty, filling lunch. And educational.

We sat back, and picked at our teeth with toothpicks that came from a little jar to be found on every restaurant table in Taiwan. *"Xiaojie!"* Kimi shouted.

She came over. *"Yào shén me?"*

Kimi leaned across the table at me. "Ask her," he said. "My Chinese sucks."

"Ask her what?" I said. "For the check? Sure," I began reaching for my money.

"No!" he shouted. "Ask her for our fortune cookies."

I had no idea how to do this. But I'd learned the word for sweet, and the word for bread. What could go wrong? I tried.

The waitress grimaced. Jake laughed. I tried

again.

"*Méi yŏu*," said the waitress. Don't have. She gave Kimi a frown and walked away.

"Sucker!" Kimi said, pointing at me. "They don't know what a fortune cookie is, yet they think they're Chinese!" His guffaw rattled the windows, drawing stares from other diners.

I paid the bill. We bid adieu to Kimi.

On the walk back, I asked: "What the hell, Jake?"

"Yeah, he's a kick, right? Oh, the fortune cookie thing. You know they were invented in San Francisco. Nobody here knows what he's talking about. And no, they don't do fortune cookies on the mainland, either."

A week later, when Jake and I sat down at the restaurant for another lunch, we learned from the waitress that Kimi had been arrested again. He'd kicked his neighbor's cat and sent it to the vet.

Life on the new frontier.

FRANCE & TAIWAN

Dealing Arms

In 1997, in an outdoor restaurant deep in the Dordogne region of France, we savored our dinner entrees. The late summer dusk sky reflected blue-orange. The air was brisk and warm at the same time, and the redolence of hearty food aromas was deep country French.

I was working on a wild boar cutlet doused in a light red sauce, while my wife was dipping enormous prawns in a thick buttery consommé, and both Chris and Hailey had ordered the grouse, a whole bird each, bathed in a port wine reduction.

It was an all-out assault on the senses. The chef must have been divinely well-connected, as the smells seemed piped in from heaven. The presentation was a sight for sore eyes, almost daring the diner to look and not touch the plate, lest they spoil the visual artistry of colors and textures. The flavors, all of them, as we passed samplings around to each other, were indescribable bliss. The textures and mouth feel—

"Ow," said Hailey. "Oops. Think I got a pebble in my bird."

She carefully worked it out of her mouth and into her napkin. She held it up to get a better look. I could see from across the table it was no rock. "Ha! It's metal."

"It looks like your bird," said Chris, "was taken down with a shotgun. Mine, too." He pointed to a shot pellet on his own plate that had fallen out of the tender quail meat of its own accord. "This region is all about fresh, wild game meats."

That triggered a memory for me. I flashed back to my year in Taiwan, a decade prior. "I guess the tubular business was banned."

"Now what in hell," asked Chris, "are you talking about, Jenkins?"

"Allow me to explain," I suggested. And as the food and wine had tranquilized our better judgements, they did.

******

"This is all under deep cover," Stan had said as we entered the lobby of the Taipei Lai Lai Sheraton, a swank hotel in the heart of the business district of Taipei. "Not a word to anyone."

Stan was from Utah. He'd been in Taiwan for a decade, first as a missionary for the Latter Day Saints, and then as a businessman. "Mercenary," was the word he used to describe his occupation. He was a hired gun, broker, trader, and entrepreneur. In a very short time I'd learned a lot about business from Stan. He was the boss. When he said "mum's the word" my lips were sealed.

The hotel lobby was opulent. There were soft pile rugs, tasteful murals that crawled ostentatiously high above us, perfumed air, and an immaculately tailored staff. That is to say, they were stylishly dressed, coiffed to a tee, and all gracious smiles.

We met Chung in the "pit" which was a bar, coffee shop, and restaurant combo, spacious with well-separated circular tables and plush seating. Light orchestral music wafted through the space, imparting the sense that discrete conversation would not carry.

Chung greeted us with a smile and deep bow. He was a small man in a large suit that looked expensive despite its ill-fit. He had a scar that made me wonder. It ran from somewhere in his mop of gray hair across his left temple and diagonally across the left eye. It continued across his nose – creating both an upper and lower nasal domain – and his lips.

The upper lip had stitches that had not benefited from realignment, making his mouth misshapen. The white of scar tissue continued onto the right side of his face, almost a straight line down from the corner of his mouth, plunged down his neck and disappeared under his collar.

Stan had brought me along on the premise that he needed technical product expertise. The subtext was to enlist more help on a crowded field of opportunities he couldn't fully absorb by himself. I'd read all this to mean he was a natural-born mentor, and unsparing in his willingness to train.

Taiwan had become a major manufacturing economy, building a huge proportion of what Japan was now too busy – and expensive – to build. Need a product? Taiwan could build it, quickly, inexpensively, and with high quality – even when Taiwan wasn't quite sure what the product was.

We sat together and got down to brass tacks.

"Let's start with the tubular business," suggested Stan.

Chung reached into his bag. "I have a sample." He pulled forth a dark metallic tube, and passed it with both hands. "Machined to your specifications. I believe you will find this to be an excellent tube."

Stan received it with both hands. It was perhaps six inches (15cm) long. He held it up, rotated it. I could see it was hollow down the middle. A tube, or pipe. He put an eye to one end and grunted in satisfaction. Then he passed it to me.

It was solid. I eyeballed it lengthwise as well. Faint rifling marks on its interior illuminated by the bar's high ceilinged lights confirmed my suspicions. I knew what this "tubular business" was all about. I nodded appreciatively to Chung and surrendered it back to him. He and Stan exchanged several minutes of rapid-fire Chinese.

"Good?" asked Stan. I realized he was asking me.

"Excellent," I said. "A well-crafted tube."

Stan nodded. "Let's talk about the rocket business."

Chung smiled. "No sample," he said. "Sorry. Too big. Here, I have some photos." He revealed several large black-and-whites. "This rocket is very inexpensive and the production rate can be thousands per month. I think we can, with a very small cost increase, create a version that is reusable."

"Um, that's interesting," said Stan. "Cost is very key for this project. It's a single-use application. Let us chew on this reusability idea."

"This is a solid-propellant rocket?" I asked.

"Of course," said Chung. "We could perhaps make a liquid-fuel version, in the future."

"For the rocket," said Stan, "we need shipments very soon. There is an urgent deadline. When can you ship 1,000 pieces to San Francisco?"

"No problem," said Chung. "We can ship in three weeks."

Stan nodded in approval. "How about the knife business?"

Something in Chung's posture caught my attention. He put the rocket photos back in his bag. I sensed he wanted to talk further on this project. In any case, he pulled forth a sample of the knife business.

He presented a wooden box with a finely carved logo, "WinTalk," which was Stan's company brand. He opened the box. The blade shone and sparkled under the lights. It was a beautiful, quality piece of cutlery attached to a hand-tailored black grip. He placed the box on his lap, and delicately lifted the knife out and rotated it for our viewing. Then he offered the dagger to Stan. "Please hold carefully."

"Magnificent," Stan said. "Would you mind if I studied this for a few minutes?"

"Please," Chung said. "Perhaps Mr. Tim and I can stretch and get us all some snacks?" He gestured to the bar's open snack buffet.

We got up and strolled over. Chung picked up three small snack plates, handed me one, and smiled as he began rummaging gently, using a pair of silver tongs, among the steaming egg rolls and *cha shu bao*.

"It looks very good," I said.

"It is delicious," he said. "Glad to meet you and to know you help Stan and me to grow our business together."

"Thanks," I said. "Truly, I'm new to this, so it's

191

you and Stan who are helping me."

"You know," Chung said. "I really admire Stan. So knowledgeable. However, I'm surprised by these projects."

I was, too, I thought. But I had my orders, so I asked: "How so?"

Chung put the tongs down and looked me squarely eye-to-eye. "I trust Stan. I know he is honest and ethical. Yet I worry about the rocket business, and the knife business. Maybe I've watched too many American movies." He laughed.

This struck me as odd, because I wasn't worried about those businesses at all. I was, however, a bit apprehensive about the tubular business. My lips remained sealed.

"Mr. Tim, are you a soldier?"

"No," I answered. "Are you?"

"Yes," he said, and traced the white scar with his index finger. "Where do you think I got this?"

"An enemy bayonet?" I suggested.

Chung's face tightened into a grimace. "No. A simple shaving accident." Then he slapped me hard on the shoulder.

"Ha! That's what I tell my kids. I fought on the continent. I cannot tell you the name of the war. It's not in the history books yet. I became a prisoner. I hated being a prisoner, so I escaped. The enemy hated *that*, so when they caught me the second time, they used something very much like that—" he gestured back to where Stan was still studying the knife, "—to teach me a lesson."

"My gosh," I said. "It must have been a very cruel enemy."

"No," said Chung. "Just an enemy. I believe it's

the same in every war. I don't like war, and I don't like weapons, but I trust Stan. Here, let me give you two more of these." He put a few more dumplings on my plate. "Let's go back."

The rest of the meeting was relaxed social talk while we snacked and finished our beverages. Stan and Chung agreed on delivery schedules for the knife and rocket business, and Chung agreed to make a slight engineering adjustment on the design for the tubular business. We parted with formal, deep bows to each other.

"What do you think?" asked Stan, as he maneuvered us at high speed through Taipei's dense and temperamental traffic.

"He seems to be a solid partner," I said. "He asked me some questions."

"You didn't tell him anything, I hope?"

"Of course not," I said. "I don't *know* anything."

"Good," said Stan. "Now, just to be clear, we are not doing anything illicit here. No illegal arms dealing. I just want that on the record."

"I didn't think we were," I said. "Chung told me has great faith in you as an ethical partner. But if you don't mind…"

"Look," said Stan. "First of all, we're brokers here. We can make deals because we know the market. Chung doesn't. He respects that. In time, he and the rest of this country will figure out the markets, and they will not need our services to keep their factories humming. We'll have to move on to other markets, sooner or later. I vote for later, if you don't mind."

"I'll second that," I said.

"The knives," continued Stan, "as you've probably guessed, are for the biker market. For some reason, folks who spend ten thousand on a Harley need a gorgeous twelve-inch blade strapped to their shins while cruising down the highway. They'll pay $150 bucks, and Chung can build them for $25, including that beautiful wood box. That's good business."

"That's great business," I agreed.

"The rocket is for a fireworks concession in San Francisco. They blow up, so the re-usable model won't figure in."

"That makes sense," I agreed. "I think I know what the tubes are for."

"Yes," said Stan. "I'm sure you do. Even though it looks bad, it's all perfectly legal – in France."

"France?" I asked.

"My buddy did his mission in Provence. He lives there now. One of his gigs is supplying restaurants with fresh game."

"You need a rifle silencer to shoot a duck?"

"It helps," said Stan. "You can get them one at a time, while they're on the ground, or in the water, without scaring the rest of the flock. Plus, no buckshot."

"No buckshot," I repeated.

"You don't want your customers to bite into buckshot, not when you're serving roast squab to celebrities at Cannes."

******

As darkness fully descended on the Dordogne, I

wound down my tale. We were all satiated from the food, and probably from the story as well.

"So," I summarized, "based on the buckshot in your grouse, I'm speculating that the use of rifle silencers for hunting game is no longer practiced here in France. At least, not here in the Dordogne."

"Huh," said Chris. "Fascinating story. While it makes sense, I still think you guys were dealing arms. Pass the butter, s'il vous plait."

TELECOMS

The Rigors of Travel

My first thought at this last minute news was that I'd need to pack the largest diapers made by man to abet the executive babysitting Ted would require. Crap.

"Hey," Ted added. "One more thing: I'm booking us all at the Guangzhou Marriott, so cancel whatever you got set-up." That was just fine by me. I waved smartly and went back to my office. I didn't bother cancelling the hotel reservations I'd made, I just added a room for Ted, who was officially crashing on our trip at the last minute. Let Ted figure out for himself that the Guangzhou Marriott hadn't yet been built.

A true "hands-on" executive can be a tremendous asset when visiting customers in distant lands. Customers will often respond by bringing their own execs to the meetings, and stubborn deals that just didn't want to close for the longest time can spontaneously happen.

Ted, our VP, was not hands-on. Trying to keep an open mind – maybe he'd surprise me -- I had to consider the prospect that my well-tooled plan for a major tradeshow in China might have to make nursemaid provisions for one very imposing VP Sales & Marketing.

This was 1997, and Guangzhou was still akin to the dark side of the moon. Ted was a Brooklynite who was physically imposing, even by U.S. standards. Picture an NBA center's height combined with a Sumo wrestler's proportions, if said wrestler has been stretched like bacon.

He wore voluminous tailored, monogrammed dress-shirts, out of which his chubby hands squirted. Big as they were, his hands appeared soft, like those of a baby descended from giants. The shirts were carnival tents. It's difficult to imagine that a single bolt of fabric could be equal to the task of supplying a contiguous length of cloth sufficient to cover him. Yet he had an endless supply of these – white silk, pin-striped, blue and black -- along with Armani ties long enough, that should an average man don one, they'd look like a kid playing dress-up in dad's closet.

Ted's presence didn't just blot out the sun, his voice and personality likewise filled up any room he entered, squeezing out all other egos. He'd joined our outfit just two months prior, relocating to southern California from New York, where he'd been an executive at a giant telecom company. Here, he stuck-out like a door knob on a sports car – a walrus in an aquarium tank.

At his prior company, he'd told us, he'd commanded a budget that was several times larger than our little company's annual revenue. We'd already seen Ted's spending habits were inflexibly similar to those he'd exercised at his last post.

Being a big guy and an executive certainly

justified his first-class travel habit. My own abbreviated stature made flying coach fairly painless; short people are blessed in at least this regard. And Kurt – my counterpart – wasn't much taller. We'd rough it out in steerage for the flight out to Hong Kong.

Or so I thought. Ted poked his head into my office. "Oh, hey, forgot to mention. Change your tickets. I want you guys riding with me up top in the dome."

"Whoa," I said. "That's not necessary. Plus, you know, corporate travel policy." I surfaced visions of my recent encounter with Derek, our budget-focused CEO, calling me to walk him through my most recent junket – not the part about customers and design wins; rather, his interest was bounded by the line-by-line details of my expense report.

"Well, don't worry," said Ted. "I'll handle Derek. Travel is hard, you guys ride first class with me."

Ours was not to reason why. Sweet!

The flight out over the Pacific was glorious – tea time sandwiches and cups of warm cashews, can-I-refill-your-champagne-flute glorious. Which was good, since upon landing we zoomed by rail out to Guangzhou and began four days of what I call "tradeshow madness."

Kurt and I found our booth vendor and helped them set it up. A show in China is all the chaos of a show anywhere – on steroids: missing parts, the rush to fix damaged-in-transit demos, arguing with installers in a foreign language, and the inevitable midnight run to get business cards printed, because someone always forgets theirs.

This time it was Ted. "Put Chinese on the backside of my card," he tossed in as I was about to run downstairs to the hotel business center.

"Do you have a Chinese name?" I asked.

"Yeah, no, get me one, would ya?"

Thirty minutes later, after describing Ted to the helpful business center clerk, we had his new card with a proper Chinese name for him. "He should like it very much," she said.

"Say it one more time, please."

"Wang Xiong Xiong," she said.

"Wong She-ong She-ong," I repeated.

"Good!" she said. "Remember the meaning?"

"Yes. Wang is king, and Xiong is a bear. What's the other Xiong?"

"Same," she said. "We use same word twice to make it funny. Not funny, cute. *Kě ài!* "

I laughed. "My boss is King of the Teddy Bears. He'll love that." Not that I was going to **tell** him he was king of the teddy bears. I'd make up something, like Noble Bear King. With a box of 500 Xiong Xiong cards in tow, I retreated to my room for the night and enjoyed a few hours of coma-like sleep.

The show was a blur. Kurt and I stood in that tradeshow booth eight hours straight for most of three days, meeting, greeting and chatting up innumerable curious visitors. Some were potential customers, most were not. A few were obvious spies sent by the competition. We made diplomatic and polite short work of those, granting no collateral or company logo pens. We had to ration these, especially after the first morning when a whole class of uniformed high school kids swarmed on us and we were slow in enabling perimeter defense. A box of 30 pens vanished.

Shortly before lunchtime on day one, we had a large visitor – Ted. He admired the booth and the show's busy traffic. He watched Kurt and I give a few quick sales pitches, then yawned. "I'm gonna head back to the hotel and get some work done. You guys keep fighting the good fight."

And that was Ted's contribution to the Guangzhou tradeshow. There was no babysitting required, so that was a plus. We caught up with him for dinner the first night, but he went to bed early the second night.

The third day, we wrapped up at lunchtime, a bit early. Boss's orders. We shook hands and hugged the local team that had made it all possible, met Ted at the train station, and headed back into Hong Kong, where Ted had suggested we spend a couple days of "decompression" from the rigors of doing business in China before flying back to L.A.

The hand-off of the Crown Colony from the United Kingdom to China was just a few months away. Before July 1st 1997, nobody really knew what that would mean for life in Hong Kong. It was just eight years post-Tiananmen Square, and pessimists wouldn't let you forget it.

Most folks were optimistic, believing Hong Kong's importance to China and the world economy would only grow under the "one country, two systems" paradigm laid out by the treaty. Hong Kong would be British for 150 years and for 50 years more, until 2047, it would have special autonomy. In any case, the handover was still a few months away, and tonight we'd be off-duty in the famous Crown Colony.

"Now this," said Ted, as the train accelerated away from Guangzhou, "Is the pay-off for all the hard work we've done the past week."

"Yeah!" said Kurt. "I can't wait to paint the town!" He was a former Marine. That is to say, he was a Marine, once and always. Semper Fi. Having spent some time in my backpacker days in Hong Kong, I was kind of keyed up myself. Ted really knew how to travel. A decompression stay in old HK was great thinking. One thing troubled me a little.

His use of the royal "we" in reference to all the hard work.

He was the commander, after all, my boss's boss, and like Kurt I would be a trooper and march straight into Hades at his command. Shore leave in Hong Kong? Was that asking too much? It was not. I was getting jazzed about it.

Still, my mind started to repeat the same groove, the way some people twirl a strand of hair endlessly. Ted hadn't exactly pressed flesh for three days at the booth. He hadn't pushed for executive-to-executive customer meetings. He hadn't attended *any* meetings, to my knowledge. He hadn't even offered to stand guard while we got lunch or took a pee break. Please, let the record show, I wasn't complaining at all. Still, facts are facts.

Kurt and I, on the other hand, had spent a frenetic few days. We'd smoothed out press releases, in the evenings on late night calls with headquarters, made quick adjustments on the fly, and adhered to the on-your-feet-at-all-times mandate, which was more strenuous to me than actual walking around. My memory of those days was a blur of endless streams of questions and answers, heavy lifting of set-up and tear-down, smiling and engaging with an unstoppable line of foot traffic, handshakes and card exchanges and bows, and guarding the collateral and the schwag which could vanish in an instant.

All while Ted, well, while Ted…I really don't know *what* he did. Caught up on his beauty sleep, perhaps. He was an executive. Yes, Kurt and I would both "go over the top!" for Ted. You don't have to salute the man, but you must always salute the rank. And Ted was a good guy. He just operated on another level.

The train pulled into Kowloon station, and we shuffled with our backpacks to the taxi stand. "Hey guys," said Ted, as we got to the end of the queue. "I'll take this one. Got any Hong Kong money?" Kurt rummaged in his pocket and handed over a wad of bills. "Hey, thanks!"

"Aren't we headed to the same place?" I asked.

"I'm at the Marriott, island side. Aren't you guys at the Novotel?" That last part was inflected in a way that made me think, yeah, damn, we're at the Novotel. Crud.

"Get settled in," said Ted, "grab a bite, then why don't you guys swing by later and we'll chit-chat. Here's my ride. Ciao!" He squeezed his jumbo frame into the back seat. He had a good technique – sort of backing into the cab, pushing the curb with his feet and sliding on in. He was a native New Yorker, after all.

"Hey buddy," he said to his driver. "Causeway Bay. J.W. Marriott. You know? Mare – eee – ott." He knew, and off they sped, one of Ted's giant baby hands raised to us. "Ciao, guys!"

"You got to love Ted," said Kurt, as our cab

door opened for us. "He's a man of the world."

We got to the Novotel. They let me cancel Ted's room at no charge. We checked in, tidied up, and met downstairs. Then we strolled to a metro station and rode under the bay. We wandered through the buzzing nightlife of Lan Kwai Fong. Hunger jumped us quickly, and we enjoyed Thai food and Singha beer. I noted the time.

"Let's ramble over to the Marriott."

"You mean the Mare – eee – ott," Kurt corrected.

We hopped on the metro again to a subterranean shopping mall, at the far end of which was an entrance to the Marriott hotel.

The lobby was grand, with ceilings so high above I can't now confirm that there *were* any ceilings. The lobby was almost all glass, immense walls of it, that drew the eye out onto the bay, which was lit with the bright lights of passing boats and the glow of Kowloon's millions of lights just beyond. Not seeing Ted in the spacious bar, I picked up the lobby phone.

"Come on up to suite 1066," he said. "I've got a comfy spread up here."

He wasn't kidding.

If anything, Ted's suite had a higher ceiling and the same window-on-the-world glass wall as the lobby. The bar – floating in the sky above Hong Kong bay, from any perspective in the room – was all crystal flutes and high-end liquor and wine bottles. The place was awash with leather sofas, loveseats, a high-end entertainment center, and big screen television sets – in every room, of course.

"This is crazy nice, Ted," I remarked.

Ted was splayed out on a large sofa. His arm

rested on the back of the sofa, the baby hand holding a martini glass. "Help yourselves to a drink, guys." We busied ourselves checking out all the permutations. I settled for a glass of chilled French Chablis.

"Ted," said Kurt, while mixing up a Long Island Iced Tea, "this must cost a fortune."

"Hey guys," said Ted, "let me tell you something about that. Travel is so hard, you need to chill and relax when you can. A suite like this is minor compensation for all we do."

While he might have had a good point at some level, I was compelled to check at the registration desk on our way out. The rack rate on his suite was $1,400 USD. Marriott guy and member discounts notwithstanding, the ostentation did not correlate with the actual labor expended. At least, I was convinced that our penny-pinching CEO, Derek, would see it that way. I felt cozy enough in my Novotel room – $80 all in. But it did get me thinking. Maybe travel *was* hard. I thought, maybe when I'm vice president, I'll travel in style, too.

The first day back at headquarters in California, I walked by the open floor to ceiling glass enclosing Ted's office. The door was closed, and through the glass there was Ted, stone-faced, in his big leather chair in one of his bespoke white tent shirts. Standing with his back to me was Derek, our Dutch-American CEO, arms in motion, voice clear, saying "...compliance, Ted, travel policy compliance!"

I kept moving down the hall. Finishing my business, I came back the same way 20 minutes later. Ted's door was still closed, and as I looked in he gave me a forlorn wave. Derek's arms, on the other hand, were still wind-milling. I heard him say, "And how about that forecast?"

I gave Ted my "brave face" smile and kept on moving, thinking: yeah, travel's hard, but that doesn't look like much fun either.

At my desk, I noticed an "all hands" email from our CFO. Attached was a revised corporate travel policy. That was fast. Long story short, absolutely no first-class travel by anybody for any reason and $125 per night cap on hotels.

An hour later, Ted poked his head into my office. "Hey, buddy," he said. "Derek wants the forecast. Numbers suck. Do me a favor? Pop on over to Ericsson and see if you can close one of those deals you're working."

Stockholm in the dead of winter. Rigors of travel, indeed.

STOCKHOLM

President Never

There would be no panic, though maybe some hyperventilation. It was ten minutes to "go time" and I was nowhere near ready.

The whole trip had been a hair-brained scheme With three days' notice, our VP had asked if I could "close some deals, fast" to save the upcoming quarter. My direct boss, Brent, had protested.

"Ted, the design cycle on these deals is months. It makes no sense." Ted was *his* boss, though, so I saluted and inserted my butt into a coach class seat to Scandinavia in February. I didn't need a meteorologist to inform me on weather conditions. "Cold and dark" all day, every day.

After five days of sailing down icy highways to get in front of customers, it was my last day in Sweden. In moments, I would mount a stage in front of about a hundred people and give an educational sales pitch, after which I would be whisked at high speed hundreds of kilometers to Stockholm airport for the flight to California.

Immune to stage fright, I had a rather pressing problem, one that reminded me why I would never be

.esident.

I'd awoken as usual at 5:15am. A glance out my hotel window said it was closer to midnight than to dawn. There was a deep carpet of snow out there, but it was too dark to see it.

The most critical business of the day begins with multiple cups of cold tap water chased by three mugs of black coffee from the in-room coffeemaker. I breakfasted on a half-sandwich I'd saved from lunch the previous day, and studied my seminar slides one more time. The magic wasn't yet happening, and showtime was fast-approaching.

I chugged more water, put on my shorts and t-shirt, and went downstairs to hit the gym. Stiff exercise often helped loosen things up. Forty minutes later, sweat-stained, I returned to my room. Still no luck. All stimulus, no yield. I breathed deeply. No panic.

Not yet.

******

Consider, as I've done, the following thought experiment: pick any modern president or prime minister. Choose one you love, one you find disagreeable, from any political party or persuasion; it doesn't matter. Choose a male, female, from any ethnicity or religious disposition, from any region of the world. For our purposes, any will do. Dictators excepted, please. Nothing personal, but they don't play fair as regards our challenge.

Now, take your chosen top elected official, be it Obama or Thatcher, Merkel or Carter, and ask yourself this: "Could I do that, hour to hour, every day, for years?" Put yourself in their shoes. Of course, you *could* be a better leader. Of course, you would bring newer, better ideas to governing, but can you *do* what they do, every minute of every day, fulfilling the relentless demand of the very public role expected of you?

I once outlined my own campaign for U.S. president. I studied ballot requirements for all 50 states – they're not that challenging – and drew up a platform that addressed more than 30 important positions: foreign policy, trade, economic revitalization, immigration, healthcare, guns, abortion, and civil rights. I was driven not so much by vanity but rather a dearth of what I believed were viable candidates entering the race. Plus, my kid asked me to run, twice. That's the definition of pressure.

Before I ambled too far down the campaign trail, I performed the above thought experiment. I imagined early morning coffee at the Resolute Desk, the daily intelligence briefing just completed, scanning the newspapers. My chief of staff would join me to discuss the day's schedule: greet the visiting president of Brazil, hold a 90 minute press conference live on national television, and hop on Marine One to Maryland for a veteran's event.

It was only 7:05am on my first imaginary day, when the hand of the Goddess Epiphany gently slapped my forehead. What had I been thinking? This wouldn't work. I reluctantly withdrew my candidacy. Epiphany, having ceased her physical assault on me, smiled brightly and said, "Being qualified to be President, yet not wanting the gig, is a sure sign of intelligence."

I might or might not be *qualified* to be

̣sident, but the very public, very structured duties scuttled my presidential ambitions.

******

Ready or not – I wasn't – the show must go on. I adjusted my tie, shrugged into my suit coat, and descended to the lobby, where I met Gunnar, my sales rep for Sweden. "Are you ready?" he asked.

"Nearly," I said. "Just a moment." I jogged down the hallway toward the loo. Movement was building deep inside my digestive tract.

Oh, how I wished this was China and I could access a squatter. Human beings evolved performing this activity on our haunches, optimizing the channel opening, permitting nature to take its course. With my combined insight into the hazards of Crohn's Disease, evolutionary posture, and Asian toiletry, I should have been first to patent the "Squatty Potty" (as featured years later on "Shark Tank"). It's a simple step stool that fits next to a sit-down toilet to simulate squatting.

Tip: once mounted on the throne, toes on floor and ankles up will mimic a squat and provide better channel alignment. Yet, now, two minutes of concentrated exertions yielded naught. What was coming would have to come later, but experience informed me that it would not be *much* later. It was show time. I scrubbed hands, took a deep breath, and took the stage.

The audience was attentive, and even granted a few courtesy laughs at the right places. From the back of the room, Gunnar eyed me warily, having seen my discomfort. After many campaigns together, he knew my foibles well. Being "on" in front of a live audience is pleasant for me, and that distraction helped. Somehow, I wound through every slide without faux pas. At last – applause! -- the ordeal was over.

I shook hands and chatted with a few attendees who approached me at the podium afterward, but took advantage of the first diversion – when Gunnar began answering a question on my behalf – to repeat my jog down the hall.

The plumbing had begun to groan now, a bit of pain that is standard for us "Crohnies." On this attempt my efforts were rewarded with a potent, gaseous emission, which effected a staccato sonic echo. It was progress, of a sort. Yet soon the levee would break, not quite now, and my flight was not going to wait. I had to keep moving.

"Good news," said Gunnar. "Johannes and Fredrik are also traveling. We will give them a lift to the airport and continue discussions."

This ordinarily happy news hit me like a nuclear bomb. I would be trapped in a fast-moving vehicle surrounded by deep snow for the better part of two hours. "Great. One more pit stop for the road."

Gunnar's worried eyes bore like lasers on the back of my head as I sped off. I accelerated through another round of noxious emanations, ignored the ominous echo from every porcelain and tile fixture, made tidy all that required tidiness, and raced to join Gunnar and company in his Audi.

Anxiety is a familiar friend for victims of Crohn's. Hyperventilation *can* help, but is not socially indicated. Pain and pressure surged, mounting over a three-minute cycle and fading briefly with the prehistoric rhythms of human peristalsis. I tried, from my shotgun seat, to ensure my grim jawline was not too obvious to our customer passengers behind.

I couldn't conceal my discomfort from Gunnar. He did a fine job, keeping the conversation going, in Swedish, which let me off the hook to focus. League after league of empty white snow drifts and scattered groves of pine trees flew by.

"Hmm," I said after an hour, seeing the first buildings that had come up in a very long while. "Wonder if we might make a pit-stop there?"

Gunnar obliged. "It's a government facility, but maybe they let you in." The door was unlocked and a uniformed guard attended the lobby. I explained my situation in English, and he graciously stood with a rattle of keys and led me upstairs to what was obviously a non-public restroom – without a squatter, of course.

Yet again, my efforts fell short of delivering the needed outcome. There were planes to catch, including my own. I thanked the guard on my way out, sucked in a bracing cold breath of winter air, and re-entered the hell-on-wheels that was Gunnar's Audi.

I watched the road signs with trepidation. Eight-eight kilometers, then forty-two. Not long now.

Then, without warning, fracture lines appeared in the dam. It was going to collapse.

The pain intensified as the channel began to part and deep inside there was seismic disruption. It gave every indicator of cresting to an irresistible force. My right hand gripped the car door handle with a ferocity that numbed my fingers.

Extreme urgency now attended my recurrent

calculations. What was the probability of leaping out and running through the snow to a spot where my activity could go unwitnessed – though my cohort would certainly know, and Gunnar would do his best to laugh it off as a stomach flu that had been bothering me throughout the trip.

Visualizing a successful scenario proved impossible. The snow was too deep to run through, and there were few trees, only wide open, flat spaces.

I resolved to go down fighting with a dash through the snow, rather than succumb in an airtight vehicle belted to an expensive leather seat. I opened my mouth to ask Gunnar to stop the car.

Nothing came out. I closed my mouth and waited. The pressure abated. Through the mystery of circadian vicissitudes, my system had decided now would not be quite right. The cracks remained, threatening, and persistent pain was their warning of impending cataclysm, yet I felt a run through the snow might yield nothing. I remained ready to shout for a quick halt, and grimly watched the road ahead. Short, shallow breaths helped. Breathe in, breathe out, repeat, faster, repeat.

Twelve kilometers. Three. Hope was a distant ray of light on the horizon, but it was there, and it was growing. Flights of random thoughts often distract me in these incidents, and my mind was now hooked on the phrase, "Politics is the art of the possible."

At last, the Audi pulled up curb-side at the terminal. Yes! It *is* the art of the possible. I staggered out of the vehicle, received my rollaboard as Gunnar handed it to me from his trunk.

"You'd better run for it, Tim!" Gunnar said. "Your flight is almost due!"

He had saved my life and I fled with just a wave over the shoulder to Johannes and Fredrik. Vesuvius was erupting and the race out of Pompeii was brutal. I dashed hundreds of meters before finding a men's room. I burst into it, only to see two men waiting and a single stall with the door closed. I turned to race on to the next restroom. The *whoosh* of the single toilet flushing as the door was closing gave me superhuman courage. I performed another about-face.

"I'm terribly, terribly sorry," I said in English. The two men may or may not have understood the words but they certainly understood the message. One looked at me, then at the other man, who waved me forward. The stall door opened, another man emerged, and sputtering thanks I jammed in, tossed my laptop bag to the ground, dropped my trousers and within seconds had completed the most critical business of the day.

It shall always remain so. I'm sure the two men, waiting patiently, appreciated my subordinated gasp of achievement. I completed the paperwork, emerged, and thanked both men profusely. They laughed pleasantly, having done their good deed for the day. As I scrubbed up, the one still waiting said, "You were *lucky* today."

He was absolutely right. Being lucky every single day for four years of highly-visible public prominence struck me as expecting *way* too much.

And that, my fellow Americans, is why I shall not seek, nor shall I accept, nomination to be your President.

SOUTHERN CALIFORNIA

The Eagle's Claw

"I want that forecast," Derek, our company CEO, said to me. It was a very reasonable request.

To what did I owe this honor, being several echelons below the exalted corporate leader? He was saying it over the phone. I knew he was in his office, a few hundred meters from mine. I had to pull the receiver from my ear and give it a critical eye before responding.

"Derek, I hear, I get it, and I understand. Shouldn't you be asking Ted?"

Ted was my boss, technically my boss's boss, and Derek was Ted's boss, after all. This was deja vu, it had been going on for weeks, even before I'd been ordered to Sweden by Ted to sweep up business that might save the quarter. Derek would drop into Ted's office. He would ask for the forecast. Ted would grunt something affirmative, and Derek would smile, give a jaunty wave, and disappear. Us sales pukes had given Ted our numbers weeks ago, so he had all the data.

After one of these impromptu reminder sessions from Derek, I'd turned to Ted and offered to integrate it for him into concise slides.

Ted, his voluminous tailored white shirt puffing as he moved, had extended his hand in a gentle 'stop talking' gesture. He was a big, gruff man with a thick Brooklyn accent. Barely three months with the company, Ted was still an enigma. A big company exec now in a small company, he'd been the dominant force in every meeting. Yet recently he'd grown soft-spoken. Come to think of it, he'd been fairly quiet since getting reamed by Derek for taking us all first-class to a China tradeshow.

"Really," I said. "It's no trouble, Ted."

He shook his head no. His jowls were Nixonian and reiterated these motions in cheeky hysteresis. "Don't worry about the forecast," he'd said.

I'd obeyed that order before, and what happened? Ted had turned around and shot me off to Sweden in mid-winter to dig for design wins. Now the CEO was badgering *me* for the forecast our boss was sitting on. I stepped next door to my boss's office.

"Oh, hey," said Brent, "how many purchase orders did you collect on your Swedish boondoggle?"

"All we predicted," I said. "Zero. Worthwhile trip, but the pay-off can't help this quarter. Now Derek is on *my* ass for numbers."

"Don't cry," said Brent, "I've been getting the same call every day you were gallivanting with the Swedes. Ted's got the numbers, guess he just doesn't want to hand them over."

"What do we do with this?" I asked.

Brent stood up and took a few paces to the right of his desk, then a few to the left. "You're a fan of military history." Brent was ex-Navy.

"You know it," I replied.

"So you understand chain of command," said Brent. "Shipboard, we swabbies had a saying. 'If it moves, salute it. If it doesn't move, paint it.' And in this case, our superior, Ted, is still moving. A bit. So we have to salute. The alternative is sticking our toes into the gears of the command chain. Ever do that, on your bike?"

The day my bare toes were threaded between the sprocket and chain of my yellow Huffy came to mind. Brent was spot on: don't mess with the chain.

"Yeah, sure," I said. "So does that mean we do nothing?"

"Not necessarily," he said. "But we have to work bottoms-up, respecting the command chain. Come on, let's check in with the big guy."

We entered Ted's office. He was tapping a pencil on the desk, huge polished shoes up on its surface, and gazing at his whiteboard, which was completely empty except for one corner: "Trade Show in Guangzhou, China," followed by a big checkmark. And below that. "Forecast," which did not have a checkmark.

"Hey, Ted," said Brent.

"Hey, guys. What's up?"

"We were wondering," said Brent. "We're getting a lot of calls from Derek about the forecast."

"Don't worry about Derek," Ted said, again making the 'don't go there' gesture.

"Um, OK." Said Brent.

"Ted," I added, "He's really pushing. Do you want help integrating the numbers?"

"Forecasts are bullshit," Ted responded.

That one caught me off-guard. From Brent's

quizzical expression, it probably knocked out his lights, too.

Forecasts *are* bullshit, no quibble there. They're creatures of pure prediction conjured under duress. Sales people cannot win with forecasts, which is why the great ones do the best they can but don't get emotionally invested in the damn things. Forecasts are one part trend-line, one part macro-economic wind, one part wishful thinking, and seven parts hubris. It's fair to call them bullshit.

They are, however, **necessary** bullshit. Forecasts drive factories, labor resources, machinery allocations. They guide the supply chain – how much of this and that to order on a vendor's crazy 8 or 12 or 16 week lead-time.

Unfortunately, they are the only thing the CFO cares about. That and expense reports. CFOs need to know the numbers so they can file the quarterly report, prepare data for the CEO to yack about on earnings calls, and drive the company's stock price; higher, if possible. If not, a story of "soft market" or "re-building quarter" needs to be spun. Hiring, firing, buying, reporting, bonuses and executive career tracks all depend on the forecast.

Sales people get this, even though our interest is correctly focused on maintaining customer esteem. Still, the forecast is the most important bullshit any sales team generates.

"Look, Ted," said Brent. "We've got the numbers. We're driving to bump 'em up. Thomas is back east working Motorola and Tim just seeded half of Sweden, but we should go conservative. We'll put it together for you; let's get some numbers to Derek and get him off your –"

Brent stopped abruptly as Derek, smiling as always, appeared like a phantom in the corridor behind the glass wall of Ted's office, and waved to us as he approached the wide open door.

"Back!" said Derek brightly.

It wasn't clear if he meant "I'm back" or if he'd heard Brent and was completing his sentence. "Since you guys are all here, how about that forecast?"

Brent leveled his gaze at me. I do not claim to be a telepath, yet I heard his voice in my head saying "chain of command." Well, then, being lower down on the chain got me and Brent off the hook.

Neither of us can be blamed for the long awkward silence that followed. It was long and awkward. I said that again to help communicate just how long and awkward it was, which leaves plenty of time to also mention that it seemed interminable. Interminably long, interminably awkward. Interminably interminable.

Ted's huge, shiny black shoes were still perched on his mahogany desk. He was still tapping the pencil. He acknowledged Derek's request only with a single off-beat pause in the pencil tapping, and perhaps a slight head swivel, maybe a millimeter down and back up again. Then the tapping continued with its same Morse code like cadence. Perhaps he was tapping out "SOS." Here-be-peril.

Yet, Ted did not appear to display any other signs of distress. He just kept tapping.

Derek – whose furrowed brow and distracted scratching of his prematurely gray scalp might have been signaling his *own* distress over the lack of any feedback from this room of people whom he commanded – now wrapped himself with both arms and began to sway back-and-forth. He glanced quickly from Ted's face, to Brent's face, to my face.

To my profound relief, Ted began whistling tunelessly. It wasn't very loud, so I didn't risk exhaling. Yet.

Derek remained in the doorway. He was a proud man. He was particularly proud of his multilingualism and seldom let us forget that he spoke five languages. At the moment, he wasn't speaking any of them. The silence ran. There should be a stronger term than 'awkward' for moments like this. I looked to Derek, then Ted, then Brent. Chain of command.

The rhythm of Ted's pencil marked out time and the taps along with his ambling whistle were the only sounds. At last, Derek cleared his throat.

"Sorry, did I interrupt something more important?"

Ted did it again. That gesture. The big hand of "stop talking." Derek read it; no doubt he'd seen it before. Ted made a show of putting his shoes back on the floor and standing up, smoothing out his shirt sleeves. "Not at all," he said at last. "Let's talk forecast."

You could cut the relief in the room with a chainsaw. Brent, Derek and I exhaled as discreetly as possible as Ted grabbed a black marker pen and approached his infinitely welcoming white board.

Ted drew a black line from left to right, horizontal to the floor. "Our trailing numbers are not bad." He wrote "$21M" above the line. He then carefully placed the tip of the pen in the middle of the line, and drew another, this one going up and to the right at a 45 degree angle. He put the marker tip at the same starting point and drew another line going *down* and to the right at 45 degrees. The line down was labeled "$18M" and the line going up was designated "$24M."

He stood back to admire his handiwork. It looked like this:

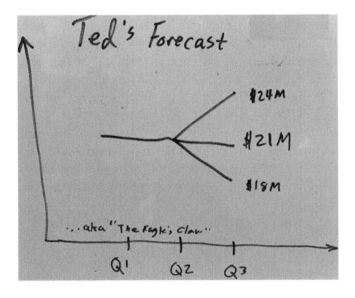

"So," said Ted. "That's your forecast." He capped the marker pen, smoothed out his shirt sleeves, and sat back down in his chair. He turned to face Derek.

Watching Derek's face closely, I could see his puzzlement trying to resolve itself. I figured he was thinking, *ok, and…? Shouldn't there be more to say about this?*

"Ted," said Derek. "Shouldn't there be more to say about this?" *Eureka!* Perhaps I *am* a telepath.

"Yes," said Ted. "There is more. The x-axis is

time, and the y-axis is revenue. In millions of dollars. U.S."

Again, you could cut the silence but you'd now need a much, much **bigger** chainsaw.

"Ted," started Derek. "What…what **is** that? Is that supposed to be a, uh, an **eagle's** claw?"

Eagle's claw! This term triggered for me the memory of the Desert One failure in Iran, when President Carter had ordered a rescue mission for the American embassy hostages in Tehran. It had been code-named, "Operation Eagle's Claw" and had ended in tragedy when a U.S. chopper had collided in the darkness with a C-130 aircraft at the desert rendezvous staging point. Eight Americans had died, and the hostages had then been dispersed across Iran so no further rescue attempts could be mounted. Eagle's Claw had become synonymous with 'complete fiasco.'

"Sure," agreed Ted. "Eagle's claw, if you like."

This statement was followed by yet more silence, a perplexing, vexatious silence.

There, apparently, was Derek's forecast. There were no part numbers, no product families, no customers, no market tiers or segmentation, no assumptions, no risks, no mitigations, no prime movers, quality and supply caveats, no "BoMs to explode" (operations lingo for Bill of Materials multiplied by number of units forecasted, etc.). There was none of the data that the CFO – and all the other functions of the company, in fact – need to weave their own plans and narratives.

To me, it did look a lot like an eagle's claw.

"That's your forecast, Derek," Ted reconfirmed. "If we hit some speed bumps, we may be down around 18 mil; we do well, we might knock it out of the park at 24. I'd go with the 21 mil, if I were you, Derek. That's a good number to show the board. That's a number the Street will like."

Derek looked at Ted. Then he turned to Brent. Brent had his hands carefully folded on his lap, his face expressionless. Then Derek's gaze shifted to me. Eye-to-eye with my boss's boss's boss. "Chain of command," warbled my hindbrain. I quickly folded my hands.

"OK," Derek said. "OK. Alright. *Alrighty* then, could I get one of you to put ... to put that *thing* on a slide for me?"

"Sure, Derek," said Ted.

Derek gave his usual salute, minus the de rigeur jaunty flair. He wheeled about and disappeared down the corridor.

"We'll put the slide together," said Brent.

Ted smiled. He tapped his pencil twice in rapid succession.

"Eagle's claw," he said. "I like that."

When the company posted the $21 million, the Street *hated* those numbers. Our stock plummeted.

And later, when the quarter numbers finally came in at $15.7 million – far short of the weakest eagle talon, and missing the forecast by a whopping 25% -- our stock accelerated into the pit and never came back, ripped to shreds by sharp eagle talons.

WUHAN, CHINA

The Wuhan Worm

The planned China Ground Campaign was just days away. "Do we gamble on the weather?" asked Dutch.

"Perhaps now or never," I said. "We're ready. Conditions are favorable. Every day of delay widens the window for our adversaries."

"Review the battleplan," said Dutch.

"We've laid out a pincers movement," I said. "Blaze and I spearhead the assault in the north," I pointed to my wall map of China, decorated with brightly colored stick pins, cities with "target-rich environments" – lots of customers. "We'll slice through Shandong province. You and Ken land here," I pointed to Hong Kong, "and open a southern front at Shenzhen. We'll divide any opposing forces."

"Hmm," said Dutch, whose real name was seldom heard. We were not soldiers, just military history buffs and tech geeks planning a sales mission.

"Ambitious," said Dutch, scratching his closely cropped brown hair. "Forcing opposition onto a two-front scrimmage with a small force is risky.

Perhaps an artillery strike before hitting the beachhead."

"Close-in air support on your left flank," I said, "will be provided by Dave. He'll soften up targets of opportunity here in Guangzhou."

Dutch rubbed his hands together. "Excellent. What's the plan for the link-up?"

Dutch and I shared the same heritage of classic World War II movies in our youth. I maintained the "Ground Campaign" metaphor. He seemed to appreciate it.

"Here," I pointed at a small cluster of pins stuck in a central metropolis. "The key to any successful ground campaign in China has always been Wuhan. The Mongols knew it, the Japanese knew it, and our competition knows it. Blaze and I will encircle from the north, while you and Ken bring up the southern pincer.

"Dave will feint into Sichuan province," I tapped my pencil on the central interior city of Chengdu, "then complete the encirclement by advancing due east. The jaws will snap shut at Wuhan for the final push on the fiber optic R&D centers. We'll take purchase orders wherever possible, and carpet bomb using dense formations of marketing collateral in preparation for a follow-up offensive before the weather turns."

"Hmm," said Dutch. "'The general who plans judiciously need not fear the outcome of a thousand battles.'"

"Sun Tzu," I remarked.

"About the little matter of prisoners," said Dutch. "Given our fast flanking action, they may slow us down."

Ah, yes. Kampfgruppe Peiper's fateful conundrum at the Battle of the Bulge. His orders: speed the armored columns to Antwerp and take the port. He'd made the decision to liquidate P.O.W.s of the American 9th Army, rather than slow the advance. Eighty-four G.I.'s had been massacred.

"As always," I reminded Dutch, "with regards to prisoners, we operate strictly within the confines of the Geneva Convention."

"Hmph," he said.

"Thus," I clarified, "taking prisoners is *optional*." I felt that was scandalously ambiguous. Prisoners could always be disarmed and set free.

"Ha!" said Dutch. "General Jackson's amnesty plan. Well played. Overall assessment? Do we have a soft 60?"

He meant do we have at least a 60% chance for success.

"Definitely a soft 60," I said.

"OK, execute to plan."

With that, I made plane reservations for five people whose real job was to sell chips — not potato, rather, semiconductor chips. Half our ten person company would be deployed. This would be a decisive engagement.

The Ground Campaign was on.

Being just weeks with the company, I was learning in "firehose" mode. Blaze and I checked into our first encampment, in Shandong province.

"Talk to her in Chinese," Blaze suggested in a conspiratorial whisper as we approached the check-in clerk at the hotel. She was a fetching young woman with a blue blazer and sunny smile. Her nametag read, "Janet Fan."

"*Nǐ hǎo,*" I said. Unsure beyond that greeting, I improvised. "*Wǒ men dào le.*" We have arrived.

The young woman's eyes grew wide. "My goodness!" she breathed. "You speak Chinese!"

"No, no," I said. "Only a little."

To which she gave a little gasp. "Great!"

We served up our passports.

"Wah!" she said, "You're American! You live here in China?"

"No," I said. "Just here on business."

"You speak clearly!" A door opened behind her, and in came another woman with the same bright smile, and nametag that read "Amy - Manager." Janet said, "I wish I could learn English like you learned Chinese."

Amy said: "If he's your boyfriend, then you will learn English quickly."

Janet's face flushed. "This is our guest!" she said. "Stop that!"

"Are you married?" Amy asked me, then pointed to Janet. "She's single, no boyfriend." Janet gasped and gave her friend a civilized, solid push on the shoulder.

"Stop it!" Janet said.

Blaze turned to me, grinning. "You did it!"

"Did what?" I asked.

"The Thirty Second Girlfriend!" said Blaze. "It's the stuff of legend. Few can hope to achieve it. You went from zero-to-girlfriend in 30 seconds! And you did it without saying 'I'm a big Janet Fan.'"

Poor Janet got redder. "Don't worry about him," I told her. *"Tā fēng le."* He's crazy.

"Truly awesome," he concluded. "Just don't do that when Dutch is around."

Over dinner, Blaze explained why. "Dutch is super easygoing — loves classic movies, certain Irish rock bands, and when not designing chips he loves goofing. He's fun to travel with. But Dutch is kinda sheltered."

"Sheltered?"

"He didn't date much. Wife is his high school girlfriend. They're serious about church."

"Got it," I said. "All I did was speak Chinese to our hotel clerk. At your suggestion."

"And great job!" said Blaze. "Maybe too great. You'll see. Dutch can get outside his comfort zone quickly, especially in China."

"Hmm. Sounds like you've seen this happen."

"Shenzhen," explained Blaze. "Last year, a quick nightcap in the hotel bar. There were three young ladies sitting nearby, looking at us. I gave them a big smile. Boy, was that a mistake. They were smiling back. Dutch got real fidgety. He still had half a mug of beer but stood up, mumbled 'big day tomorrow.'"

"So," I asked, "Dutch doesn't subscribe to your 'sleep is optional' view?"

"Oh, heck no," said Blaze. "He's very disciplined. What was strange was him walking away from an unfinished pint. He loves beer, and he's thrifty."

"Guess he'd had enough," I surmised.

"Guess he'd had," Blaze agreed. "Anyway, we strolled to the lobby, elevator opens, we get in. The darndest thing, the three ladies came in right after, like they were following."

"Maybe they'd had enough, too."

"Sure," said Blaze. "But Dutch was freaking out. His face was purple. I tried not to encourage them, 'cause I knew this was not a good scene for Dutch. But hey, I need to be charming."

"You can't help it," I confirmed. "Beyond your control."

"Exactly," said Blaze as he prodded the platter of stir-fry with his chopsticks. He lifted a wad toward his mouth, and most went in. A bit dropped in a ballistic arc, landed on his coat lapel. He didn't notice. I reached across with a clean tissue to attempt triage.

"Thanks," he said. "One lady asked me a question. Which, I have to say, was very unsettling for Dutch."

"Uh oh," I said.

"Yeah," said Blaze. "First, she asked *me*, and I shook my head negative. Then she asked Dutch. You know what she asked?"

"Well," I said. "I can only imagine."

"She asked if Dutch wanted them to come to his room. Not one, *all* of them! Dutch was completely spacing!"

I had to hand it to Blaze. This was a very amusing vignette. "What did he do?"

"He said 'No mas!' Then he sort of tried to hide in the corner of the elevator, but he's a big guy. When the doors opened at my floor, I stepped out, but he yelled 'Wait!' So, I got back in, the doors closed, and up we went to his floor. Awkward!"

"The ladies felt it too," continued Blaze, "and left him alone. But they hadn't pushed an elevator button, so...they were clearly just along for the ride."

"I hope you escorted Dutch safely to his room."

"Oh, no," said Blaze, "he wasn't taking any chances. At his floor, we stayed on and pressed the lobby button. We all rode straight back down in perfect silence. I began whistling the Jeopardy tune, trying to lighten it up. Back downstairs, the doors opened, and I knew what to do."

"What was that?" I asked.

"I followed Dutch off the elevator, waited for our entourage to emerge on our heels, then shook hands goodnight with each. That got lots of giggles, and they headed back into the bar. I'd never seen

Dutch so uptight. We got back on the elevator, this time no hot pursuit."

"Alright, then," I affirmed. "When we get to Wuhan and catch up with the gang, no Thirty Second Girlfriends."

"That would be best," said Blaze. "But make no promises! You, too, must be charming. It's a force of nature."

"Ha," I scoffed. "Not *my* nature."

Two days later, Blaze and I landed at Wuhan airport, and boarded a taxi. The pincers of the Ground Campaign were closing. Wuhan is a huge, sprawling city cut in half by the mighty Yangtze River, and the airport is well out of town. The summer sun was fading behind a dirt-yellow sky as our driver tore down the highway, intent on passing every other vehicle on the road, and making liberal use of his horn to that end.

Wuhan stank. It smelled, sure, but stank in the sense of mad sprawl and disorganization. It reminded me of the vast urban wilderness of Los Angeles. We passed huge sectors of mid-rise apartment buildings interspersed with endless factories and industrial parks, a university here, a steel-and-glass sports arena there. A few buildings could easily have served as a Bond villain's complex of evil-doing.

The city is a true crossroads, and is centermost in China for research and development in fiber-optics, communications, networking, military weapons research, and biological sciences. Being at crossroads, Wuhan combines old world populations from across China with modern students and professionals. Its open air food markets – now globally infamous for including "wet markets" – are rich in diversity, with something to suit every taste, from shark fins to turtle eggs. A friend who lives there brags Wuhan has the most deliciously crunchy crickets – roasted, salted, peppered, sold in paper bags, hot and ready to eat on the go.

We arrived too late to explore any open air dining and coincided at hotel check-in with Dutch and Ken, who'd traveled with Winston, our in-country sales representative, on their relentless advance from southern China. That bit of precision timing was *not* part of Ground Campaign planning, but it impressed the boss.

"Excellent synchrony," said Dutch. "Now we can launch a provisioning raid on the local eatery."

"First guys," said Winston, in his cockney accent, "let's get your stuff upstairs." He handed out keycards. "I'm afraid you're in adjacent rooms, sorry about that. If you hear pounding from next door, it's not me. I'm two floors down. Ha-ha!"

Dutch's ears went florid.

"Ha!" said Blaze. "Sleep is all we need."

"We'll eat downstairs," said Winston. "They have great fare." Winston was Hong Kong born and raised, and Oxford educated. "After we sup, there's a fabulous club in the basement where we can get a proper drink and relax a bit."

"Great!" said Ken. "Any live music?"

"Lively tunes de rigueur," said Winston. "Can't guarantee a band, but a talented DJ is certain."

Dutch's ears had normalized, and he rubbed his hands together. "Excellent," he said. "Most excellent."

The food, as promised, was great – spicy chicken, claypot lamb – with just a dash of more exotic cuisine. Perfect for hungry troops on the march. Our conversation focused on the strategic customers in Wuhan we'd see tomorrow.

"Where's Dave?" asked Winston.

"Dave got flow-controlled in Chengdu," I informed them. Sadly, everyone who flew in China knew this term. Commercial flights had multiplied so fast that for years the air traffic control system, now among the best in the world, was overwhelmed. "Flight delay due to flow control" announcements were most dreaded, and all too frequent.

"Best to pivot," I said. "He'll fly direct to Shanghai and I'll link up with him there."

"The finest battle plans are obsolete," said Dutch, "once the enemy is engaged."

Time for that "proper" drink. We five piled into the elevator. "Missing Man formation," quipped Dutch, "in Dave's honor." He demonstrated the formation with his hands, making jet plane noises.

"Nice!" said Winston. "We'll party plenty to make Dave proud."

The elevator doors opened. It was dark, a black velvet tunnel, with floor lights guiding the way. The club staff, all females dressed in satin black tunics and mini-skirts, were equipped with a light clipped on their collars, illuminating faces and shoulders. On our left, greeters bowed welcome.

To the right was a large open room with elevated bleachers, five echelons. On each bench sat a dozen or more youthful, winsome female staff.

"Wahhhh…" said Winston.

Blaze shouted "Hi everybody!"

"Hey, Winston," said Dutch, "we've got an early morning."

"Of course," said Winston. "We'll just have a few drinks, sing some tunes." Winston turned to the maître d' and began exchanging information in low tones.

Her smile was bright as Winston outlined our request, which included beer and music. Beyond her stretched a long corridor with many doors on either side. I thought it strange that there was no sound coming from that corridor; no music, no clinking glasses. Could we be the first customers of the night? The *only* customers?

The maître d' turned smartly and waved us to the first room on the left. Inside was a huge leather sectional, seating for a dozen. In the center of the room against the entryway wall was a large flat screen and on the left was a karaoke machine, flashing like a pachinko parlor in Tokyo. There were drink tables laid out with numerous studio-grade microphones. In all four corners of the room were shoulder-height black speakers. The place was wired for sound.

We made ourselves comfortable. The beer arrived driven by another satin-dressed woman pushing a hand truck, four racks of 12 each bottled Heineken.

"Um," said Dutch, "We don't need that much."

"That's the minimum order," explained Winston. "We can make a big dent." The woman began opening bottles and handing them around. "See, we've already started! Cheers!"

"We can do it," said Blaze, who emptied the first beer in seconds, then picked up a microphone, stepped up onto a drink table. He belted out, "Borrrnnn to be www-iii-lll-ddd!"

"Yeah," said Winston. "Will sound better with music."

The maître d' left, and another young woman entered to tune-up the sound system. Blaze gravitated to her. "Got any Steppenwolf?" She showed him the English music collection. "Hey! House of the Rising Sun."

The maître d' now returned, and with her came another black-satin young woman, followed by another, and another, and another, and….

"What's all this?" asked Dutch.

"Wait," said Winston, who was watching the procession closely, beer in hand. "There's more." The room was big and it was filling up fast. When finally it seemed no more women could fit into the room, they stopped.

"What's happening?" asked Dutch. "Why are they here? We're just going to sing. Just singing, right?"

"Of course," said Winston. "We each choose two girls—"

"Negative, ghostrider," said Dutch. "The pattern is full!" His ears were scarlet. "No, no, we're just singing."

"That's right," assured Winston. "And if you don't like any of these, we can dismiss them and bring in more."

"No girls," said Dutch. "Only singing. Winston, what are you trying to do here? This is karaoke, KTV, it's just for singing. I don't want to sing in a sort of … *brothel*."

"Whoa!" said Winston. "Dutch, these young ladies are not here for that kind of thing."

"No? Then what do they want from us?"

"These are our back-up singers," said Winston.

"Hey, great idea," said Blaze.

"Back-up singers?" asked Dutch. "I don't do Tony Orlando. No back-up singers."

"Come on, Dutch," said Blaze, "We're Gladys Knight. We might need some Pips."

"Choose any two you like," reminded Winston.

Dutch was bolt upright on the leather couch. I had the impression that, given a pathway, he would catapult out of the room. But the door was blocked by an army of black-clad female back-up singers.

The maître d' took matters into her own hands. She clapped once and the women began filing out of the room.

"You OK, Dutch?" asked Winston. "Buddy, you look like you've seen a ghost. I understand these weren't suitable for you."

"Roger that," confirmed Dutch, taking a deep breath and a swig of beer. "Not in the least."

"Don't worry," said Winston. "Problem solved." And in charged another group of women.

"What now?" said Dutch. "What's happening?"

"We're seeing a different selection," said Winston.

"No," said Dutch. "We're *not*! Cease fire! Tell them to stop! Repeat, no back-up required." Yet, on they came, the room was filling fast.

Now it was clear. Winston leapt up and exchanged words with the maître d'. She gave the same single clap, and the flow of "back-up singers" suddenly about-faced and began filing out.

Yet the maître d' was none too pleased and she waggled her finger in Winston's face. It seemed she expected to maximize revenue on the room our merry band was occupying, and that included retainer of a significant number of her staff. As back-up singers, of course.

Winston turned to us. "Anyone want a back-up singer or two?"

We all declined in deference to the boss, but Dutch took no chances. "No, Winston. We came here to sing and to have a beer. Maybe 48 beers, but *no* back-up singers. Do you copy?"

"Gladys Knight only," said Blaze. "No Pips, they're leavin' on the midnight train."

When Winston reported this news, the maître d' became very animated. *No* was not an answer she would take. She pushed back, no doubt pointing out that it was Frankie Valli *and* the Four Seasons. She and Winston argued and haggled without seeming progress. Finally, he turned back to us.

"She says ok, no back-up singers. But we must accept a DJ."

"A DJ?" asked Dutch.

"Yes," said Winston. "She says normally we would have to pay for at least ten back-up singers *and* a DJ. We must have a DJ."

She clapped and yet another troop of women began to file in.

"No!" said Dutch. "Whiskey Tango Foxtrot!—"

"Just choosing one for DJ," said Winston. Your choice."

"Reverse polarity!" said Dutch. "Disengage!"

"No problem," said Blaze, "I'll choose our DJ. Is it ok to ask them a few questions first?"

Now it was Winston's turn to say, "No! Just pick one."

Blaze, ever unflappable, closed his eyes. He pointed his finger and spun round in circles, once, twice, three times, stop! The women had a good laugh at that. The "chosen one," having tried to duck from his little game of spin the bottle, gamely stepped up to the equipment as the others filed out.

"Let's start with The Animals," said Blaze. "That means Tim is up!"

It's the only song I can sing without greatly annoying an audience. The guitars reverberated off the walls. I stood, grabbed a microphone, and began.

"There is….a HOUSE…in New Orleans….they call the Rise - ing Sun!"

There followed whoops of gaiety. Hey, maybe I *was* a force of nature. Later, Blaze compelled me to be his back-up singer for "Sweet Caroline," but thankfully the whole group pitched in with the "BAH! BAH! BAHHHHH!" Dutch started to relax on his third beer and did an impressive rendition of U2's "Where the Streets Have No Name." We did make a good dent in those 48 bottles of beer, leaving no more than a six-pack when we wrapped-up at midnight.

I slept well, rose early, and met Blaze, Ken and Winston for breakfast. "Dutch isn't feeling too good," Ken reported. "He's going to pass on chow."

At 8:00am, Dutch loaded himself into the van. "You didn't sleep well?" asked Winston.

Dutch grunted. At the customer site, he looked like the walking wounded. Yet he snapped into action when the technical questions came. Toward the end of the meeting, he quietly excused himself to visit the latrine. Thirty minutes later, we were running out of idle chit-chat with the customer when Blaze, who'd performed a number of surveillance overflights on Dutch's status, returned with good news.

"I encouraged him to 'fire for effect!' Looks like bombs away. It helped that he was able to exfiltrate on multiple fronts."

"Impressive, Blaze," I said. "Great use of military lingo."

"The Wuhan Worm," said Winston. "Sorry about that. The runs and vomiting tend to be simultaneous. Many foreigners get it first time here. Good news, it tends to recede quickly."

Our commander-in-chief had become the first casualty of the Ground Campaign. A Purple Heart not from direct combat or friendly fire, but at the "hands" of a miserable little worm.

"Dutch," I said, "are you requesting Dust-off?" – the term for evacuation out of theater.

He shook his lead. "Got to lead from the front," he said. "Let's press on."

"Sure you don't want us to call for back-up?" suggested Blaze.

Dutch smiled thinly. "Reinforcements, Blaze. Stick to the jargon. Anyway, *back-up* is not authorized. I'm still queasy."

The Ground Campaign was a resounding success. Never before in the course of our corporate endeavor had so few done so much for so many revenue dollars.

CHICAGO

Million Dollar Moniker

"*Ach, scheisse!*" moaned Otto, folding his face into his open palms. Was that a ***tear*** on his cheek? The poor guy was literally crying into his beer. "My life is destroyed. *Das is Alles!*"

"Whoa," I told him from my side of the big team dinner table. "Easy, aren't you over-reacting?" But Otto just rubbed his hands on his shaven scalp, eyes vacant. I glanced at Joachim, next to him. He was a fellow countryman of Otto's, and ***he*** was smiling. The big news didn't seem to upset Joachim. "See, Joachim is ok," I said. "It's obviously not so bad as your worst fears."

Otto faced me. "My worst fears? *Mein gott*, you mean Arsemann? *Scheisse!*" His head collapsed again.

"You know," said Joachim, still smiling, sweeping his thick blond hair into realignment. "It ***is*** actually. Our new company name is far, ***far*** worse than Arsemann."

Oh. Well, I thought. Then it had to be really quite awful indeed.

This is the tale of two German salesmen, one American marketing woman, and thousands of their fellow employees, who came together in a "merger of equals" that promptly began searching for a new corporate identity, so that it wouldn't have to remain "Newco" forever.

Otto had grown up in an open, well-ordered democracy at a time of great prosperity in his native Bavaria. He'd studied engineering and gone to work fifteen years back for NanoQuad, a U.S. company.

For Otto, life had been predictable. He'd scored high marks in school, and his career had run on a smooth rail as he achieved great success in building relationships with customers and selling a line of high-tech products that year-on-year progressed and never failed to "wow" his customers in central Europe.

Joachim, on the other hand, had not grown up in a well-ordered progressive democracy. He'd grown up in post-war Dresden, East Germany, in a neighborhood that, thirty years after the end of World War II, still had bullet-scarred low-rise tenement blocks, unreliable electricity, but plenty of hot water – assuming one could find enough wood to heat the water over the kitchen's open fire pit.

Joachim's life had *not* been predictable. He'd started school, then was forced out to perform child labor in a factory when his father – a doctor – had been sent to prison on charges of "excessive capitalist tendencies." Several years later, he'd been put *back* in school after his father was released from prison, a happy side-effect of German reunification. Joachim quickly caught up, studied electrical engineering, and found himself working as a technical sales engineer for a German company which was later bought by an American company, FM-NSAA.

The dinner we were now all sharing was to mark another unifying event. Otto's company, NanoQuad, and Joachim's company, FM-NSAA, were merging. "Sort of a second marriage for us," Joachim had joked earlier in the evening. "Otto and I became fellow countrymen at re-unification, then fierce competitors, and now we're to be joined at the hip as comrades."

"I'm not gay," Otto had protested, laughing. "*Und bitte*, I'm uncomfortable when ex-communists call me comrade."

There were twelve of us at the big table in one of the finest steak and seafood restaurants in Chicago. It was the eve of the biggest industry show of the year for our business. While our two companies would still operate from two separate booths this one last time, due to SEC clearances still in process for the corporate merger, all the major customers from around the world would be present. The final merger was just weeks away.

I looked up and down the table. In addition to Otto and Joachim, another German, Ryker, represented the Frankfurt design center for our product lines. Also present were Caitlin and Cooper, from Philadelphia, our sales rep from Israel, Ilan, our Czech-born UK salesman, and our man in Paris, plus Kenzo from Japan and Feng from China. Then there was Blaze and I.

For months, since the merger announcement, we'd been meeting and planning for specific strategies to merge our two product lines and sales efforts, while at the same time continuing to compete with each other – all around the world. From our customers, the most frequently asked question was, "What's the new company name?"

Well, we wished we knew. And with the big tradeshow about to open in the morning, Cooper was checking his phone minute-to-minute for announcement as promised of our shiny new corporate identity, so we'd have something to tell our customers tomorrow morning.

"That was Margarita's promise," said Cooper. "A promise is a commitment not to be broken, not in ....well, not in our new company, whatever it may be called."

And now our tale switches gears to the marketing person, Margarita. She wasn't just NanoQuad's VP of Marketing; she had also won the bake-off of merging organizations and was the new VP Marketing of the entire unified entity. Margarita was a polished executive, mid-30's, all high-energy, charisma, and panache.

She had traveled over the previous months to all the facilities of the two companies, meeting, greeting, and collecting ideas, not just for a new corporate identify, but a new corporate *essence*. When she'd visited us in California, she'd told us:

"This re-branding effort is critical to our combined company's future. As NanoQuad, we had great success with the re-branding I launched three years ago."

Blaze, unprompted, had volunteered to remind everyone present of the slogan that Margarita had released back then. He jumped up, and said: "Reach Far, Grab Hard!"

"Yes," said Margarita. She paused. Her expression had changed, almost like she was hearing her own slogan for the first time. "Yes, and it communicates to customers that with NanoQuad their reach is increased and their confidence in our products allows them to take the bull by the horns. As it were."

As it were, indeed. Widely respected throughout the company, Margarita had the additional characteristic of being something of a magnetic beacon to admiring eyes – with long red hair, Helen of Troy cheeks, and attire that leaned toward the "Oscar Night" side of business formal. She commanded phenomenal levels of charisma.

"She's a marketing goddess," Blaze had noted. Having joined NanoQuad well after that unglamorous choice of nom d'plume was a fait accompli, Margarita had applied herself brilliantly to sharpening the corporate image wherever possible. Her branding sensibilities ran to the edge, maybe a little beyond the edge, at least for a geeky hi-tech company.

The "Reach Far, Grab Hard" slogan had been controversial in the roll-out, but customers either didn't notice it or thought it was a bit racy in a good way, giving the company's mundane products sorely needed sex appeal.

Cooper had summed it up like this: "Margarita knows how to slap lipstick and a tutu on a pig and make it sizzle like bacon."

Now, with full command of the combined marketing machinery of two great companies – both burdened with mediocre names – Margarita was outspoken about changing the game. There was a lot at stake, after all. NanoQuad and FM-NSAA were dreadfully boring even for tech companies, and all indicators were that no hint of either legacy name would appear in the newly minted nomenclature. Margarita's email updates to all hands hinted strongly at an "invented" corporate name, a "Xerox" or "Accenture" style pastiche detached from any existing word.

In business school, I'd learned such exercises could be fraught with peril. The much delayed rollout of our new moniker – which had been decided weeks earlier, and was a closely guarded secret – implied the vetting process wasn't easy.

The pre-eminent business school "lesson learned" in this regard is the mistake Coca-Cola had made in its first attempt at a Chinese name. The marketing geniuses at Coke had worked diligently to choose Chinese characters that it deemed helpful in selling sugary fizz water in a land of tea drinkers, while sounding very much like Coca-Cola in spoken Chinese.

There may have been some confusion in respect to *which* Chinese spoken language was the right target. One theory is that Coke relied too heavily on Cantonese speaking consultants. In any case, the unfortunate result was a character set that translated from Chinese to English as…

Bite the Wax Tadpole

Though by some kinder interpretations, it may have been…

Bite the Wax Cowboy

And, by *less* favorable interpretations, it may have meant…

Lady Horse Stuffed with Wax

Kodak.

That's what I say to that. Kodak. Although now a shriveled husk of its former self, they chose wisely by creating a name that could be uttered by anyone on the planet and yet did not – to our current understanding – *offend* anyone.

Chinese Coke sales fell flat. The company quickly corrected, a foreshadowing of their excellent handling later on of the "New Coke – Coke Classic" near-disaster. They came up with a fresh set of Chinese characters that not only sound better, they literally translate to…

Taste Good Happiness

Now *that's* solid branding. With that correction, much sugary fizz water was sold in China.

For our "merger of equals" Margarita had spoken of her goal of combining several themes in the new name.

"Our new company," she'd proclaimed "brings together the voices of thousands in *chorus*. NanoQuad and FM-NSAA, once bitter rivals, will sing together in perfect harmony."

Hmm. Again, that made me think of Coke and its eponymous 1971 "rainbow" song in which folks the world over (to the extent this was enabled by Central Casting) expressed a strong desire to "buy the world a Coke." Very promising.

"Together," Margarita had continued, "we bring a ***developing core*** of technologies from which great products are built. Our technology core is therefore paramount. And," she'd added, "our technology core itself is a focus of ***beauty***, like a diamond glinting in the sun." And finally, she'd resonated on a marketing parlance that has since overtaken the technology world.

"United, we travel, journeyers on a ***voyage*** of discovery. Our new company is not a destination, but rather a journey."

And so, therein lay many clues, but no answers. The atmosphere of our team dinner was flush with expectation. The veil of mystery was about to lift.

Now seated and served with our first round of drinks and appetizers, I sensed building team spirit. Folks were having fun, and tomorrow we'd be in front of customers and no longer gunning for each other, but cooperatively selling the full combined portfolio. Up to a point, of course. And still pending final SEC approval. Just saying.

"Otto," said Cooper, from across the table. "You look nervous. Cheer up!" To which Otto responded by leaping out of his chair, beer glass in hand, grin set to max.

"Not at all, Cooper!" he said. "I have the greatest confidence in our marketing geniuses and overpaid consultants." That drew laughs. The watchword was that $2.5 million had been spent in the search, refinement, and vetting of our new corporate brand. "I want to propose a toast. To marketing!"

All stood. "To marketing!"

"Cooper is right," said Joachim. "No need to be nervous, my comrade in arms."

Otto rolled his eyes. "No? Maybe you're right. If you give *me* a lousy $10,000 I could pull a great name out of my ass."

"Yah," said Joachim. "And it will stink. That's what they did two booths down from us, you know."

"What's that?" Blaze asked. "Are you talking about TriGyn Technologies? Sounds a little too gynecological, I think."

"No, no," said Joachim. "TriGyn's marketing people are true professionals compared to who I'm thinking. Maybe you guys didn't notice?"

Ryker held up his hand. "I know. So does Otto. Come on, man, say it!"

"Arsemann," said Otto.

"I'm sorry?" said Cooper.

There was much merriment at Otto's glum face. "Arsemann, Cooper, *Arsemann*! There's a fucking company that named itself Arsemann."

"It's technically the owner's name," said Joachim. "Friedrich Arsemann Rudiger Traunstein. You know, if you have a catchy name, sometimes you might want to use it. Nobody who knows Arsemann will forget." Joachim was all grins. "Although, I think he'd have done better with just his initials."

"Now," said Otto, "do you see why I'm nervous?"

"Comrade," said Joachim, "let me get you more beer. Everything's going to be fine. Margarita will make you proud, she has searched the world for the chorus, the voyage, and the development core, maybe even something about Vikings rowing together to a lusty drumbeat."

And it was all fine. The food was first-rate, the conversation light-hearted. We were into desert. I glanced at my phone. Still no announcements. It was getting late. Would we have our new name by morning?

Joachim was in the middle of a very funny story about one of his favorite customers, when he excused himself. "*Entschuldigen*," he said, holding up his index finger while reading a new message. He took a sip of his beer as he read, whetting lips for the continuation of his vignette.

It was not to be. His eyes grew wide. His mouth formed an "o" and there was a sharp intake of breath.

"Oh…I'm…so sorry," he repeated. Then he stood, gripped Otto's chair, bent over, and, in the parlance, began to bust a gut. His laughter conflicted with the act of breathing. He was quite uncontrolled.

On the opposite end of the table, Cooper had also received an important message. "Hey," he said, "you got it, too, Joachim? It's from Margarita. Ok, guys, let's toast. We have a new corporate name!"

At last, the waiting was over.

I looked at Joachim, still bent double, holding onto Otto's chair. "No, Cooper," he waved weakly in protest. "Some of us," he halted, panting, giddy with guffaw, "…are not ready yet to hear it." He pointed at Otto from behind, and shook his head, mouthing "*No*…."

Otto said, "What is it? Ach, *mein Gott* already, tell us!"

Cooper raised his glass. "Ladies and gentlemen," he declared. "Welcome to our new company. Welcome to DevCorava!"

Some survivors of the nuclear blast at Hiroshima reported that, seconds before their world changed, the city fell silent. Even birds in the park stopped twittering. After a brief hush, everything was different.

At Cooper's announcement, we experienced a similar phenomenon. An eerie silence. Followed by a cacophony of sounds generated by our new reality.

Next to Cooper, I saw Ilan, our Israeli sales rep, drop his head onto his palm, producing an audible *slap*.

"What?" said Kenzo. "Did you say DevCora—"

"Acchhhh!" said Otto. The table fell silent again. We were all looking at Otto. His eyes were wide as saucers

"Phhhoooft!" came a strange sound from Ryker. My German is weak, but I believe he wasn't speaking. Rather, that was the sound of wine being shot between his lips back into his glass.

"No, Cooper," said Ryker, wiping wine from his mouth. "Perhaps you said it incorrectly?"

"No," said Cooper. "It's DevCorava." I heard a gasp from my left. Pascal, from France, was also wide-eyed. Cooper continued: "I like it. It's got the development, the course, the core, the chorus, the voyage, whatever. Everything Margarita promised. DevCorava."

Otto was on his feet, face red. ***"Stop** it! This is **not** funny. Joachim! Let me see."* Joachim handed over his phone. Otto read the message from Margarita. *"Ach, du lieber!"* Then he slumped back into his chair. "Is this October Fool's Day? Is there such a thing? This is not *real*."

"It doesn't sound so bad," said Blaze. "Plus, it's versatile. You can shorten it to 'DevCa.'"

"No," laughed Ryker. "That's actually even *worse*."

And this is where Otto moaned, and collapsed his face into his hands. "It's a joke, right?"

Joachim, who's smile had not faded, put a friendly hand on Otto's shoulder, and gave him a very gentle, reassuring pat.

"Verflucht!" Otto whimpered.

"He means he's screwed," said Ilan.

"I can't face them tomorrow," said Otto. "Maybe, I just can't face them *ever*. It's all over for me."

"Whoa," I told him. "Hang on, Otto. If Joachim is still smiling, whatever DevCorava—"

"Verflucht!" said Ryker.

"---whatever it might mean in Europe can't be all bad. It's obviously not so bad as your worst fears."

Otto glared at me. "My worst fears? *Mein Gott*, you mean Arsemann? *Scheisse!*" His head collapsed again.

"You know," said Joachim, cheery as ever. "It is actually. It's much, *much* worse than Arsemann. And, in deference to Caitlin here, I shall explain the problem as delicately as possible."

Joachim began by defining Central Europe, at least as far this new name was concerned.

251

"Everything German speaking plus Poland, Hungary, Czech, Serbia, Greece, you get the idea. And Israel."

"Yah," said Ilan. "I am also *verflucht*."

"My whole world," moaned Otto.

"Mine too, comrade," said Joachim. "This new name, nice as it might be, sounds much like a common slang word used in the region. Actually, it sounds like **two** slang words both meaning the same thing, put together. And both these particular slang words attach, shall we say, to a certain caliber of social worker."

"*Achh!*" blurted Otto.

"Maybe not the right term, social worker," continued Joachim. "It means a type of female worker who provides certain services on a short-term basis."

"A masseuse?" asked Blaze.

"Yah," said Joachim, "perhaps a type of masseuse. One offering more focused services."

"*Verflucht!*" muttered Otto.

"A prostitute?" asked Blaze.

Caitlin laughed.

"Hmm," said Joachim, "Yes, certainly a prostitute. Not just any kind of prostitute. The kind who markets their services much like a street vendor."

"Oh, you mean a hooker," said Blaze, helpfully.

"*Ach du lieber!*" said Otto, pounding the table, rattling the glassware.

"Yah," said Joachim, "Certainly a street hooker, but one with a particular quality."

Even Blaze didn't dare offer help on this one.

"Let's see," said Joachim. He took a deep breath. "How shall we say. A DevCorava is an enterprising woman. Who works as a street hooker, with an exceptional quality."

"Auf!" said Otto. "I want to die. *Now!*"

"What?" asked Blaze. "What exceptional quality?"

"Yah," said Joachim, "She, this DevCorava, is a street hooker who is absolutely, bottom line, no questions asked, the *lowest cost* service provider one can find."

Everybody was now laughing. What choice did we have? Everyone, except Otto. His arms were on the table, one coat elbow was dipped in leftover apple pie à la Mode, his face buried, shaved head rocking slowly back and forth.

"Looks like I spit in my wine," said Ryker. "I'm getting more. Anyone want more wine?"

"So," said Joachim, massaging Otto's shoulder, "there is some good news here, perhaps. Maybe it's not all so bad. Our new company name has all the development core, voyage, chorus, whatever. Yet, it also expresses that we offer something our customers truly treasure. *Great value!*"

Caitlin, the only woman at our table, clapped her hands together smartly. *Bang!* "That's right! Come on guys, cheer up! And yes, Ryker, let's have more wine. We're going to *clean up* with this new name."

Turns out, she was right. The next day most customers – those from anywhere outside Central Europe – thought the name was fine, and they liked the "chorus" "development core" and "voyage" stories that went with it.

The European customers? Why, they were having a *hoot* with us.

"You guys are so hilarious," said one from Poland. "I can't wait to see product boxes show up with *that* stamped on them."

Another, from Russia, had ribbed: "Hey, Otto, when I tell you I need a better price from now on, I expect you to perform. Ha ha!"

When Margarita caught wind of this minor little challenge, she was non-plussed. She sent out yet another all-hands *rah-rah* email that reiterated the story and even leveraged the "great value" concept. She was utterly fearless.

Today, that logo ships out on many thousands of boxes and the company has grown substantially. Bold marketing, with all its perils, can pay off in a big way.

We'd offered customers a bite of the wax tadpole, and they'd found it tasty.

If you enjoyed this book, leave a review on Amazon, and check out its predecessors:

Missions Accomplished and some funny business along the way

And

More Missions Accomplished and a lot more funny business

Connect with Tim

missionsaccomplishedpress.com

missionsaccomplished@yahoo.com

http://missions.uniiweb.com/

Amazon Author Page:
https://www.amazon.com/Tim-Jenkins/e/B07B2L9PGN?ref=dbs_p_ebk_r00_abau_000000

Where to next?

Made in the USA
Las Vegas, NV
25 February 2021